Deliver Us From Temptation

Deliver Us From

TEMPTATION

Tony Turner

with Barbara Aria

THUNDER'S MOUTH PRESS

NEW YORK

Published by
Thunder's Mouth Press
54 Greene Street, Suite 4S
New York, NY 10013

LIBRARY OF CONGRESS CATALOGING IN PUBLICATION DATA
Turner, Tony.
    Deliver us from temptation : the tragic and shocking story of the
Temptations and Motown/Tony Turner with Barbara Aria.—1st ed.
        p.   cm.
    Includes index.
    ISBN 1-56025-0348
    1. Temptation (Musical group)   2. Soul musicians—United States—
Biography.   3. Motown Record Corporation.   I. Aria, Barbara.
II. Title.
ML421.T43T87   1992
782.42166'092'2—dc20   92-21939
[B]   CIP
                                                           MN

Text design by Kate Nichols
Set in Bodoni Book
Printed in the United States of America

Distributed by Publishers Group West
4065 Hollis Street
Emeryville, CA   94608
(800) 788-3123

To my loving parents, Eleanor and William Green,

and to

Jesus Christ,

who said, "Take heed that no one deceives you."

I give them all my love

Contents

Acknowledgments

Plead my cause O Lord, with them that strive with me: fight against them that fight against me.

Psalm 35

Before you begin reading, I would like you to share with me in thanking the following people who helped and encouraged me throughout this project, including longtime friends and co-workers, as well as new friends who I encountered as my work progressed:

Barbara Aria, my cowriter for this book, as well as for my first book, *All That Glittered: My Life with the Supremes*. Barbara continues to prove an extremely talented writer as well as a friend and confidant. She encouraged me to write about all the details, yet understood my need to write this fascinating but sometimes difficult life adventure without vengefulness or bitterness.

Madeleine Morel of 2M Communications Ltd., my literary agent. I thank her for once again being instrumental in bringing another book to life.

Neil Ortenberg, publisher and senior editor at Thunder's Mouth Press. I applaud him for having the strength and courage to publish this book. His advice and guidance were right on target, and that has made it a pleasure to work with him and his staff.

Dan Levy, my editor, for his careful and sensitive fine-tuning of the text.

Frank Weimann, literary agent—for his invaluable assistance, I thank him.

Richard Barrett, manager and president of Three Degrees Enterprises, who along with his wife, Julie, has continued to guide my career with support and encouragement.

Pat Newson, my personal manager, for her devotion, her love, her prayers, and her work.

Diane Mancher, my publicist, for her continued guidance and valuable advice, always peppered with friendship.

Alfred Fariello, who once again went to the audiotapes and provided us with skillful transcription services, while extending his patience and faith.

Sherry Page, my assistant, for her uncanny insight, her friendship, and for sharing the Temptation.

My unending thanks to performers Josie Short, Nate Evans, David Sea, Robert "Boochie" Maye, Gary Kwek, and Cory Catalano for going to bat for me constantly.

Many thanks to Debbie Rhone, Mike Mullins, Billy Bannister, and Diane Showers—you're invaluable.

My deepest gratitude to my aunts Debra Sims and Betty Valesquez for their belief in me.

My sincere thanks to Lorraine and Frank Stockley and Barry Laster for opening their hearts to me.

Margarette Harvell, for her spiritual guidance.

The late Florence Ballard, the Supremes' founder, for being my constant source of inspiration.

A special thank you to the *All That Glittered* tour crew, who helped me have a wonderful time and a great publicity tour, in particular: Karen Day, tour manager; Ramona Acosta, tour coordinator; J. R. Ortiz, tour road manager; Dorinda Butts, tour assistant; Charles Johnson, security chief; Keith Collins, security director; Eugene Summers, Richard Lee, Jr., and Carlos Carmona, bodyguards.

My Tampa team—Bill Baker, photographer, and Kip, at MLD 111; Larry Montgomery and Rudy Alvarez at Hair Sensations; and my master stylist, Lenda Burton.

I am grateful to all the people who bravely expressed their private thoughts in conversation with me, but asked to remain anonymous.

Most importantly, I must express my gratitude to my parents, who sheltered me from what I call "Life Without Living," and to all the other family members, friends, and guardian angels for continuing to provide their very welcome support.

I must also openly express my love and appreciation to:

Eddie Kendrick, who taught me that doing the right thing in a world so crowded with temptations can be a tricky thing indeed.

Dennis Edwards, who taught me that when the temptation to tell the truth comes over you, don't resist it.

David Ruffin, who taught me that the art of timing, like the art of being a Temptation, cannot be learned—it can only be recognized.

Once a Temptation, always a Temptation.

Guided by the Lord, my shepherd, I remain,
Tony Turner
Gulf of Mexico
1992

Deliver Us From Temptation

Preface

Nearly thirty years ago the original Temptations broke out on the airwaves with their first string of hit records and became a household name, known to millions as the world's top black recording group. Today, that name lives on as a legend. And, largely because of what the name has come to mean, the Temptations—whether they're original members, replacements, or former members—still perform to packed houses all around the world.

But the crowds who flock to see the Tempts sing their inimitable harmonies and dance their now classic dance steps don't know the whole story. Few people understand what some of those Temptations have lived through since they sat in the cloistered security of their first stretch limos. Fewer still know what happened to three of the Tempts' lead singers—David Ruffin, Eddie Kendrick, and Dennis Edwards—as they left the group to pursue solo careers, failed, and ended up holding on for dear life to the memory of a legend that they had once helped to create.

Through my long association with Diana Ross and the Supremes
I became a friend and, later, an employee of those three former
lead singers of the Temptations, on whom this book focuses. I worked
with them through thick and thin, witnessing the sometimes funny
and often tragic events of their lives on- and offstage and listening
to their stories of Motown—how Berry Gordy, Motown's founder
and president, built them up as stars, only to walk all over them
and tear them down as people. I watched them struggle, individually
and as a group of "former Temptations," to reclaim their past stature
in the eyes of the world. And I wondered why they let themselves
fall again and again—was it all really Motown's fault that their
fabulous success was cut short and never relived, as many ex-
Motowners claim?

In writing these memoirs I went seeking answers to that question.
I looked not only at the Tempts, but also at other ex-Motown per-
sonalities with whom I became acquainted—among them, Martha
Reeves, Mary Wilson, and Mary Wells. Were they all victims of
Berry Gordy's system of star-making and star-breaking?

This book is about a legend that has gone on a long time, awfully
long. It's about what happened to the three principal heroes of that
legend as they more and more desperately chased their once-upon-
a-time, glorious, superstar days. It's an inside view of lavish lifestyles and gutter lifestyles, dissipated energies, self-destructive
tendencies, strange business practices, sex and drugs, highs and
lows, and sheer determination to succeed. Above all it's the story
of one man, David Ruffin, and his inability to resist the temptations
placed before him by a world that adored him when he was up, and
ignored him when he was down.

Many people warned me against telling this story. Eddie Kendrick panicked when I announced my plans to write about my experiences with him and the other Temptations, despite the fact that
he had endorsed my first book, about my life with the Supremes. I
found his fear to be particularly peculiar since he had gone out of

his way to proclaim the earlier book not only truthful, but also fair and even-handed. David Ruffin admonished me against divulging any sexual secrets. "Keep family secrets confidential," he suggested. Dennis Edwards warned me, once again, that truthful books can never make everybody happy. He was right.

Nevertheless, the story had to be told. I trust that as you read the following pages you will enjoy a penetrating yet honest look at the Temptations and the Motown "family," written without malice, and without trying to rifle anything or anyone out of the closet.

Chapter One
Don't Worry, I'll Always Take Care of You

It's early June 1991. I am boarding a flight bound for Detroit, preparing to say my final farewell to the man who was for all intents and purposes my "godfather," the man I called "The Voice of the Temptations," David Ruffin. Twenty-five years have passed since I first made this journey to the Motor City—twenty-five years since that summer of '66 when I cheerfully waved good-bye to my mother, leaned back in my seat, and looked forward to two weeks of fun and adventure with Florence Ballard, original lead singer of the Supremes, and the rest of the Motown family—including, of course, those temptin' Temptations whom Flo had been telling me so much about ever since I'd first met her, a year and a half earlier.

I was twelve when I first met Flo Ballard and she whisked me off to the Ed Sullivan Theater in New York so she could introduce me to her Supremes "sisters." I can still remember the day as clearly as if it were yesterday—the way she stood in the middle of a big,

5

fancy, midtown department store lobby looking so grand with all her bags and furs around her, and out of the blue sky asked me, a complete stranger, to get her a cab; the way she acted like I should know who she was, because she was a Supreme and they had just had three number-one hit records in a row. I remember thinking that Flo was just too fabulous for words because, as a kid growing up in Harlem, I had never seen anyone quite like her. But then, walking into the Ed Sullivan Theater with her for the first time, I realized that there was a whole world of glamorous, young, black people just like her—a world of women with furs and shopping bags, and guys in suits with wads of money. This was the world I was dreaming of as I boarded that plane with my suitcase full of new summer outfits and my head full of limos and mansions.

Now it's 1991, and I've made this journey to Detroit many times since that first time, twenty-five years ago, when Flo first invited me to Hitsville, U.S.A., and to the annual Motown company picnic on Belle Isle. That summer was when I really got to meet the whole Motown family. At least, that's the way the company seemed at the time—like a big, happy family of aunts, uncles, cousins, sisters who all lived in the same neighborhood or had come from the same projects, and at the center of it all was the Gordy clan: Berry Gordy, his parents, and all his sisters and brothers.

The whole Gordy family had had a hand in building the Motown machine. Pops, who had his own construction business, had literally built Hitsville in 1959 along with a crew of young singers and musicians whose time and energy transformed a former photographer's studio into a record company headquarters with its own recording studio and pressing plant. Then there were the ever-present sisters. Gwen Gordy, who'd had her own label before it folded and kind of merged with Berry's, had let his acts practice in her living room during the early days before Hitsville. Esther had been Berry's first secretary and now, as a company vice president, was in charge of Motown's management company, ITM. Her husband, a state legislator, was the company's original comptroller. Loucye, another vice president, took care of the books, while her husband arranged music for the company.

Anna Gordy was the sister I'd heard most about. She'd started the Artist Development department, hub of Motown's image-making, and had also brought handsome and talented men to Motown, including a young Marvin Gaye, whom she ended up marrying—much to the disbelief of many of the female performers, since Anna was seventeen years older than Marvin. It was a tight, sheltering, family-run business, which made everything feel kind of comfortable and familiar, as if you were simply leaving your own family to join another.

The Gordy clan was Detroit royalty, and at Hitsville the Gordy name was hallowed. Nobody said, there's Berry's sister, or there's Berry's mother. It was always, Anna Gordy, Esther Gordy, Mother Gordy, Pappa Gordy, or simply a kind of awestruck "The Gordys." Someone like Diana Ross, who always wanted to do, and get, a little extra, might say Mom or Pop, which definitely put her in a different category, as if she were almost part of the clan. She spent most of the time at that picnic flattering herself by fluttering around the Gordys, watching what they were up to and trying hard to become a part of it. Of course, by now Diana was Berry Gordy's special interest—everybody knew that. And by 1966 it was definitely paying off.

The Gordys had always done well in business, and they had always lived well. In fact, years earlier Berry's father had been driven out of Georgia because, as a cotton farmer and businessman, he'd made so much money the white people got jealous. That was how the Gordys ended up in Detroit. A lot of the people at Motown had come up from the Deep South—or at least their families had. Most of those families had come north looking to make some money working on the assembly line, and most were still praying for the day they could take a rest from it all. The Gordys, on the other hand, had come with cash and put it to work for them. Each member of the family had religiously put away money every week into a family credit union. So when Berry wanted to start his first record label he just had to go to a family meeting, like a board meeting, present his proposal, and request the eight hundred dollars he needed to get it started. The family was like a company, and the company was like a family—or so it seemed.

Berry hadn't done too well before he started his Tamla label. He'd been an unsuccessful professional boxer, had tried to make a go of a record store but went bankrupt, and then ended up working on the Ford assembly line. But he had a real talent for songwriting and he knew a hit when he heard one. Together with Gwen, he'd written some songs for his former boxing buddy, Jackie Wilson, and when some of them, like "Reet Petite" and "Lonely Teardrops," got to be hits, he thought he must finally have some money coming to him.

That was when Gordy realized that to make money in the music business you had to do the whole thing yourself. You had to control the songwriting, production, and publishing. He knew there were plenty of talented kids out there just waiting for the chance to have their songs or their voices recorded, including nineteen-year-old Smokey Robinson, who really looked up to Berry because he knew exactly what was needed to make Smokey's songs sound like hits. Gordy was thirty when he started his company—young, but old enough and confident enough to be able to mold those young singers and songwriters into stars if they were willing to listen, to follow devotedly, and to grant him control. Smokey was willing, and in 1962 Gordy rewarded his loyalty by making him a vice president of the company.

Smokey was the only Motowner who was allowed to mix performing and administration, and for a long time he was the only one allowed both to perform and to write and produce. All the other artists had to wait for Smokey, Berry, or some other Motown writer-producer, like the fantastically successful team Holland-Dozier-Holland, to want to cut a song with them.

Of course, the acts that were doing well were usually the ones that got picked. Mary Wells was the first one. When she had her first hit in 1962 with Smokey's "The One Who Really Loves You," and then another and another, it looked like she was set. Her records had crossed over—which meant that they were hits not just on the "black" R&B charts but on the "white" pop charts too. That, Berry knew all along, was the real secret of success. You couldn't afford to alienate white audiences with black, churchy-sounding voices like Aretha Franklin's. And when you had a group of determined teenage girls straight out of school, like the Supremes, or a wild bunch of guys like the Tempts, you had to polish them up real well so you could book them into the high-paying white supper clubs. It was a must.

To that end, Motown put their budding stars on a kind of Ford-style, image-making production line. The company took in kids full of hope and dreams and raw talent. They molded and scolded them—handled their bookings, managed them, choreographed them, styled their stage outfits, got their teeth fixed, taught them how to speak nicely, which fork to use, what to say in an interview, and even more important, what not to say—and then sent them out as budding stars. Motown's future superstars.

These were the days of milk and honey, the days of new houses, new cars, expensive furs and jewels. Most of these kids were coming very quickly from nothing into a whole lot of everything, and they all wanted to be picked to record the next sure-to-be-a-hit song so they could buy more, drive a slicker car, and just plain have more money.

It seemed to me during that picnic as if everyone wanted to get Berry's attention. They wanted him to look this way, look that way, look at me, look at us, look at what we're doing over here. Motown had not only planned a series of competitive sports events, but they had also organized dance-offs and sing-offs between the different groups, with each act doing a bit of whatever they were known for. Though it all looked like just plain family fun, there was really a lot of animosity behind it all—especially when some of the performers started doing mocking impersonations of one another.

Gordy had a passion for competition, and he'd use it big time. For a long time it kept everyone on their toes producing what he wanted without them asking questions about how much money they were earning, where the money was going, or where their careers were headed. They were too busy competing against each other for Berry's attention and approval to wonder who, in the end, they were doing it for.

Everybody wanted to please Gordy. They wanted to do well, and to be recognized for it. It didn't take me long to understand that the Motown stars and would-be-stars saw Gordy as their only path to success. They believed in him, and they believed that he wanted what was best for them. He was the father, the teacher, the guru, the guiding spirit who would always make the right decisions for them. He could be trusted—after all, everybody was turning out hits, and everybody was better off than they had been before they signed with Motown. Without him, they might still be out on the streets of Detroit singing on some street corner and going home to the projects, or worse.

That summer of 1966 was serenaded by Motown hits, all with that same Motown sound—"The Sound of Young America," they called it. The company had fourteen hits on the charts over the year, and they were all playing at that picnic. People had come with their portable record players that took a dozen batteries and were so big and heavy you had to stagger to set them on the table. Almost every table had one of these portables going full blast, each one better and louder than the last—everybody wanted to show that they were up on the latest purchases. And they all had their two little record-carrying cases, one for 45s and one for albums. That day, you could hear the Four Tops' "Reach Out," the Miracles' "Going to a Go-Go," the Supremes' "I Hear a Symphony," and the Tempts' "Ain't Too Proud to Beg."

Of course, I knew all the Temptations' hits. I could sing along to practically every one of their songs. Their first hit record, "The Way You Do the Things You Do," was cut in '64 after Smokey beat Berry in a songwriting contest to see who could come up with the most-likely-to-make-it song for the group. I'd heard all about the Tempts from Flo, because the Supremes and the Tempts were very close. But they were just names and voices to me—Eddie Kendrick, the one with the high, falsetto voice on "The Way You Do the Things You Do"; David Ruffin, who sang lead on the 1965 smash-hit million-seller "My Girl" and most of their other hits too; Melvin Franklin with the impossibly deep bass voice; Paul Williams; and Otis Williams.

So when I met them at the picnic, Flo started explaining, "Don't you remember I told you that Eddie Kendrick's and Paul Williams's group were called the Primes and we were the Primettes. We were their sister group—they helped me get it all started. Remember, before that I used to sing with the Primes as the featured female singer. It was Paul, honey, who asked Diana to join us." And she pointed out a slightly drunk-looking man who I'd seen acting very belligerent all afternoon. I wondered if she was thanking him or blaming him for the introduction.

Flo gave me the whole history of the Tempts—how Eddie and Paul were childhood friends and had come up together from Alabama to try and make it in the music business; how Eddie, "a mama's boy," as Flo called him, had become homesick and discouraged, and gone back south until Paul convinced him to return to Detroit; how it just so happened that just as Eddie got back to Detroit, Otis Williams's group, the Distants, had made a date for an audition at Motown and were suddenly two members short; how Otis asked Eddie and Paul, of the Primes, to join up with what was left of the

Distants, and how when Berry heard the result he signed them right
away to his Miracle label—"If it's a hit, it's a miracle." They named
themselves the Elgins, but since there was another group called the
Elgins they had to find a new name fast, and nothing seemed more
appropriate for a group with their sexy, dashing image than the
"Temptations."

Looking back at it now, I wonder how Otis Williams can claim
that he's the founding member and leader of the Temptations. He
founded the Distants as a doo-wop group when he was about fifteen.
Paul Williams founded the Primes down in Alabama. In a sense,
the Tempts was really a joint venture. Besides, the Primes taught
the Distants everything they knew—all the dance steps that Paul
had perfected, all the sophisticated harmonies that Eddie and Paul
had developed together. When they started recording with Motown
it was Paul and Eddie who switched off on leads until David Ruffin
joined the group, replacing former Distant Al (Eldridge) Bryant in
1963. That was when Paul started to lose his leads.

Even then, back in '66, I could see that Otis was just in the
background along with Melvin and Paul. Eddie and David were the
ones who people were paying the most attention to at that picnic.
They were definitely the emerging stars. And David Ruffin by that
time was making no secret of the fact that he knew he was destined
to be a huge star, because it was David's voice that had brought
them their first million-seller, and had been keeping them on the
charts ever since.

Later that week Flo took me to see the Tempts perform at one
of Detroit's most chic clubs. Motown people would always go to one
another's shows if they were in town—it was expected of them and,
let's face it, there wasn't a hell of a lot else to do in Detroit. Besides,
some of these groups had formed close friendships with one another
in a competitive kind of way. When they weren't working they'd
play cards endlessly, compare dance steps, and party together.

Of course, I was thrilled to finally see the Tempts up on a stage.

Eddie and David were electrifying together. You could see the competition between them bouncing back and forth, and their vastly different styles made it one hell of a show—quite different from the Supremes' or any of the girl groups' shows. The Temptations weren't sexy and demure like the Vandellas—they were sexy and hot! Their movements were quick, precise, and powerful. The way the guys rotated from mike to mike, it looked like they were just missing crashing into each other by a hair. David Ruffin was doing splits and flips to top even the great James Brown, and their famous, super-cool "Temptations' Walk," invented by the choreographer Cholly Atkins, always got the crowd on its feet. It was like there was a fire in the house.

When it was all over each of those guys ended up with two or three women hanging around his neck. The Temptations were, as Paul Williams used to say, "selling sex"—they worked on that with their choreography, their attitude, their delivery, their tight-jacketed outfits. They had the added benefits of Eddie's irresistible good looks and David's irresistible voice.

David had been a drummer before replacing Al Bryant in the Tempts. Originally, when Al looked like he was fading out of the group, it was David's brother, Jimmy Ruffin, who was supposed to replace him—he had even been promised the job. But one night early on, after a couple of years of hard work and no hit in sight, the Tempts appeared in some small Michigan club, and David, without any warning, jumped up on the stage with them. He snatched Paul's mike, and started singing and dancing, going down into the audience and driving the crowd completely wild. It was as if the Tempts had found the magic they needed to get them where they wanted to go. Suddenly, a very hurt Jimmy was no longer in the running to join the Tempts. His brother David was their man.

I remember very clearly meeting David for the first time at that picnic. I had on a two-piece cabana set, shorts, and matching jacket that my mother had bought for me. It was striped in weird colors

—cranberry, gray, and lime—which made me feel somewhat out of place among the suave people dressed in their best casuals. Worse still, I was carrying a bamboo harpoon that Flo had just brought me from one of her Supremes' tours, and wearing another present from Flo—a huge, straw cowboy hat. I remember David coming up and yanking my hat to the side of my head. "This is how you wear it," he said, turning up the brim. From that moment on, the hat took on a whole other look.

I liked David Ruffin right away. He was someone a kid would like, because when he talked to people one-to-one he was very cool and made them feel important. When he spoke to me back when I was young, he would get himself down to my level so we could have face-to-face contact, and he would talk to me as if I were an adult. Eddie Kendrick was like that too, although not as talkative as David. On the other hand, Otis and Melvin, when I met them, didn't give me much attention.

As I got to know them a bit better, I started to see that Melvin could be very sweet, very jovial, the kind of guy that wants to be liked. But Otis never warmed up. He seemed to always be looking around to check up on what everyone else was doing, and it didn't take me long to notice that nobody was doing anything in front of him that they wouldn't do in front of the boss, Berry Gordy—"Otis would tell on his own mother," Eddie remarked one day. Paul, meanwhile, just seemed like a drunk to me. Of course, a lot of people were getting drunk at that picnic—even I had a stolen sip. But Paul was the only one who got nasty drunk. He was rough and tough with anyone who got in his path.

Eddie came across as mild-mannered and nice, but he didn't let people get to know him the way David did. It was only later that I found out Eddie was really a shy person, a country boy who'd been so scared to death during his early days in Detroit that he developed a reputation for being the reserved, silent one. On stage, though, Eddie was the one that reached out to the crowd. David was just the opposite. As a performer he was untouchable. But in real life he was a fun guy, like a grown Dennis the Menace. The whole time we were at that picnic he seemed to have a joke, a scheme, a plot up his sleeve. When Levi Stubbs of the Four Tops sat at a picnic table having a conversation with a Vandella, David would say, "Look at those two! Them gossips, they've got their heads together—they must be talking about me." And he'd go over there and butt in and cause a whole confusion.

Flo introduced me to everyone at the picnic as her "godchild." If someone took you in at Motown they always made you a sister, a cousin, an aunt, or something like that, because this was a family and you had to belong. But Flo didn't like the big-sister routine. "Honey," she'd say, "Flo's nobody's big anything." She was fighting this supposed weight thing that Berry Gordy was always on her about, so she didn't like the word "big." "Godmother" sounded more dignified.

When Flo introduced me to David, he told me, "Well, I'm going to marry Flo one day. So if Flo is your godmother, then I'm going to have to be your godfather." I'd noticed that he was hanging around Flo a lot at that time, like he was trying to get close to her. Everyone at Motown seemed to be trying to get close to everyone else.

But I guess Flo was only interested in being David's friend. "He's just fooling," she said. "I ain't hardly gonna marry David. There couldn't be more than one star in that family, and I *know* it would have to be him!"

David, who was already married anyway, didn't pay her any mind. "We don't need no church or anything like that," he said. "I'm going to christen you right here and now." And he poured some cognac right over my head. "Isn't it 'ashes to ashes and dust to dust' or something like that?" David asked.

"No, it most certainly is not," said Flo. "That's for a funeral, fool. You're supposed to say, 'in the name of the Father, the Son, and the Holy Ghost."

It stuck. David Ruffin had made himself my godfather, and would remain so through all the years and changes and troubles to come. But back in '66 I had no idea how many changes and troubles there would be. Here was a family—my second family—and like them I just thought it would always be this way. There would always be the Temptations, there would always be the Supremes, Martha and the Vandellas, the Marvelettes. Nobody would ever die, nobody would ever break up, everyone would stay together and live happily ever after.

Looking back now, I can see that the seeds of discontent were already germinating in the summer of '66. Gordy was not running a family, he was running a business, and the whole time while he was telling people that they didn't have to worry their little heads over contracts or lawyers or accountants because they could trust him, he was also subtly letting them know that they were expendable. There were plenty of kids in the Detroit projects waiting to be made into stars. He'd proved his point when Mary Wells, after some years at Motown, a few big hits, and a high-profile tour with the Beatles in England, decided to accept a very generous offer from Twentieth Century–Fox Records that included a verbal promise of future movie contracts.

Mary was still under contract to Motown at the time, where Gordy had been pushing and polishing her with all his might, as well as pampering her with a five-thousand-dollar mink stole. In the ensuing legal battle Mary claimed that the Motown contract she had signed when she was still a minor, at age seventeen—a contract that Motown told her she didn't even need to see because this was a question of trust and loyalty and "you'll always be taken care of"—became void when she turned twenty-one in 1964. When Mary's attorney, who had been hired by the company, tried to convince her that Motown was the best place for her, she fired him and hired her own. In the end, though Motown claimed Mary Wells as their own very expensive creation, the judge ruled in favor of Mary. Motown had to release her.

Years and years later, Gordy admitted to having made a big mistake in his calculations concerning Mary. He said he should have held off releasing her big hit record, "My Guy," until after her twenty-first birthday, thereby keeping an ace in the hole. Instead, he ended up covering his losses by putting the big push behind the Supremes—three girls who had been struggling so long they'd been dubbed the "No-Hit Supremes"—and then pointing out to everyone that, as he had predicted, Mary Wells could not get a hit at Fox, while the Supremes were riding high.

Now Gordy was proving his point again with Martha Reeves—disloyalty to the company did not pay. Martha had paid her dues at Motown, biding her time as a secretary until the day Mary Wells missed a recording session and Martha stepped in. Soon, she and her Vandellas had become the number-one girl group at Motown, the group that got the best songs and the biggest push. But Martha, unlike most artists at Motown, had some previous music business experience. She started asking about where her money was going from massive hits like the 1963 "Heat Wave," and Gordy answered by pushing her group into the background. With the Supremes on the rise, he no longer needed Martha the way he once had. When Martha then started complaining that she wasn't getting good material and felt like she was being ignored, Gordy simply pushed her further down on to the B list, where Martha got even less material and attention.

In time, a bitter Martha ended up with a little band for backup, while Diana Ross and the Supremes had all of Gordy's attention and the best of everything. By 1966 everyone in the company could see that the Supremes and the Temptations and the Four Tops were the first to get everything, while the rest—the Contours, the Spinners, the Marvelettes—were constantly struggling to be recognized.

Of course, there were plenty of hard feelings when some people got pushed to the foreground while others who sang or danced just as well got left behind. I'd been watching behind the scenes the tensions between Diana Ross and Florence Ballard, and as the picnic wore on and people started having a few more drinks, tongues started to get loose and I heard a little bit of everything about everybody else too. I heard people start to argue and pick at each other, kind of in the spirit of fun, but it wasn't all fun. The bitterness and jealousies were there, eating away.

Paul Williams had become bitter because he'd sung lead as founder of the Primes but by 1966, the only solo he had left was "Don't Look Back." Eddie and David had become the pivotal figures in the Temptations. Although a lot of people assumed that Eddie and Paul were the closest because they had come north together, at this point it was Eddie and David who were close. Paul was in the middle. As I got to know them better, it looked to me like a seesaw, with two on one side, two on the other, and one in the middle ready to go either way.

But that wasn't the only reason for Paul's drinking. Apparently, he was tormented by the fact that he had fallen in love with Flo Ballard's cousin, Winnie Brown, but he was still a married man. Now, I couldn't see even then why Paul should be so miserable about this. After all, lots of Motowners were married, and it didn't seem to stop them from doing whatever they wanted. I'd heard all about Diana Ross's affairs with Smokey Robinson, who was married to Claudette, and then with Brian Holland—a relationship that came to an abrupt end when Brian's wife, Sharon, tried to beat up on Diana.

Rumors were flying about who was going with whom—there was Mary Wilson and Duke (Abdul) Fakir of the Four Tops, then you had one Marvelette, Gladys Horton, with a Contour, and another Marvelette, Wanda Young, with a Miracle. One of the few Motown stars that was not surrounded by controversial chatter was Melvin Franklin, who was reputed to be very prudish. Otis, on the other hand, had quite a different reputation. Inside reports circulated about his being so overly endowed that later, when Otis was romancing Patti LaBelle, people would joke, "I know why Miss Patti's hitting all them high notes tonight, baby!"

The joke took a turn for the worse when Mary Wilson became involved in a secret, passionate love affair with singer Tom Jones. Many said that they'd heard Tom Jones, like Otis, was extremely well endowed, and they would laughingly suggest that Motown officials would have been much happier had Mary found her passion and pleasure with Otis. However, Otis himself admits that he had a thing for Flo.

There must have been a lot of sexual experimentation going on out on the road, because as time went by nobody would think anything of asking some single girl who happened to be hanging around, say, if she was going with one of the Marvelettes, or a Vandella.

Later, when I was older and knew Eddie Kendrick better, he would ask me persistently, and usually out of left field, if I had been having an affair with Berry Gordy during my teenage years. He told me that he, and several other Motowners, had often wondered about it. They were so perverse that none of them could see why else Berry would have accepted me as an insider. Some time later the shoe would be on the other foot, when some of the same people would ask me whether or not, and for how long, I had been having an affair with Eddie Kendrick.

Gordy, of course, was in a position to have just about anyone in the company whom he wanted until Diana Ross started making her moves. Even then, Berry tried to branch out. I remember hearing a story about the night Diana came to Berry's room unexpected while Berry was busy in bed with Chris Clark, a blonde, white singer whom he was pushing, despite her lack of talent. When Berry heard that knock on his door he just shoved poor Chris into the closet, and that's where she stayed all night while Berry romped in the sack with Diana.

So, despite the ultra-wholesome image of Motown concocted by Berry Gordy, sometimes it seemed as if the company was just one big bed, which naturally led to quite a few fights and an occasional firing—like when Martha Reeves discovered that the band member she was going with was also going with one of her Vandellas. Suddenly there was a new Vandella. Wives who were left at home while their husbands fooled around on the road got jealous too. Any woman who got near Eddie Kendrick was warned to stay away because Eddie's wife, Pat, was intensely suspicious. "I'll cut your thing off!" she'd warned Eddie, and since he figured she probably would, he stayed pretty much to himself. Nevertheless, Eddie did manage the odd extramarital affair. In the early years of Motown, according to Flo, he and Diana Ross had been secretly involved. Flo told me about Eddie and Diana, and about how close they had been for a period. But, she said, in the end Diana told her that though Eddie looked like the man of every woman's dreams, his emotions were very guarded. I remembered this conversation with Flo in later years because I noticed that anyone dealing with Eddie—whether on a professional, personal, or sexual level—always had to take the backseat, even if that person was actually the one doing the driving. The exception was Eddie's wife, Pat, who was never one to mince words.

On the whole, though, it didn't seem to make any difference whether or not you were married. The only time it mattered was if you were going with someone from the outside, because Gordy hated outsiders. Once, when it was found out that Betty Kelly, one of the Vandellas, was going with a member of Anthony and the Imperials, who were not a Motown group, Betty was called into the office and asked, "Who's your favorite act?"

"Little Anthony and the Imperials," Betty replied.

"Don't say that," she was told. "Choose somebody that's in our family. There's plenty of good-looking young men at Motown." Obviously, it was not in Betty's best interests at Motown to be associating with an Imperial. I also heard a story about David Ruffin being fined by Motown for being with a white girlfriend.

Gordy hated outsiders—outside lawyers and accountants, interviewers, hangers-on—and he loved fines. Motown people, whether they were performers, producers, or even administrators, were fined for all kinds of things, including being late for meetings or performances, getting drunk, getting stoned. If a Motown executive was two minutes late for a meeting, he might be fined fifty dollars and locked out. Some of the groups even fined themselves. Otis Williams fined members of the Temptations for lateness, drinking, and dope, while Paul Williams took on the task of levying fines for onstage transgressions like messing up a dance step, or going on in a badly pressed stage outfit.

Motown had a variety of ways to keep its stars totally in the company's control. Besides the fines and the exclusion of outsiders, the most obvious was the way Motown set itself up to take care of every aspect of an artist's business—from booking and management, to recording, artist development, legal representation, and accounting. Some of those performers never saw a tax return while they were with the company. It was all taken care of for them.

It wasn't until 1977, when ex-Supreme Mary Wilson filed a complaint against the company for conflict of interest, that I started looking more closely at Motown's star-making system and it became clear to me that there had been something very wrong in the company assuming so many roles. But in 1966 hardly anybody cared about that, because everybody was doing well and nobody thought it was ever going to end. As Gordy told Mary Wilson early on when she asked about her contract and royalties, "Don't worry. I'll always take care of you."

Motown virtually acted as a bank for its artists. The Tempts, for instance, were given an advance of five hundred dollars a week each against their earnings from royalties and live performances. If they needed to buy anything, all they had to do was let Motown know, and the money would be released. If the Tempts were on tour and one of their wives needed money, she would go to Motown and tell them, "My kid needs new shoes," or "The mortgage is due," and it would be paid.

All of these expenses were deducted from the artist's royalties account, as were the expenses incurred on tours, including all the extras lavished on the stars—limos, champagne, first-class hotel suites, and the like. The Tempts were never given any written statements showing what they had earned or spent. They just knew that whatever they wanted, they could have, and since the champagne kept on flowing and the limos kept on rolling, it seemed as if they must be making plenty.

Some, however, were beginning to balk at the system. David, definitely the most worldly of the five Temptations, wanted more control. He wanted a say in the creative side of things—although the artists were charged for studio time and musicians used while the vocals were going down, they had no say in what songs they recorded, who produced them, or what was released. That was all decided in various production and quality-control meetings, from which artists were excluded. And although several of the artists were able songwriters, including David, they were never allowed to write or produce their own material. It was a form of dependency that was starting to chafe as the money rolled in and survival became less of an issue.

David also wanted a say in the business end of his career. "It's my fuckin' money," he'd say. "Nobody controls my money. Fuck that 'always take care of you' shit. Gordy better take care of me now!" He was spending plenty and living high. He bought himself a huge place in Ontario where he went whenever there was time off, just to mess around and be by himself. His favorite thing was to ride a horse by the water.

David loved horses, and he loved cars. At one point he bought a Cadillac and had it lined with mink. Back in 1966 he was driving an Eldorado convertible, emerald green with a white interior. I'll never forget it. David showed up at Flo's house in his car one day while I was in Detroit, just as Flo was sending me out to the store. When he offered to give me a ride I immediately begged him, "Oh, let me drive, let me drive!"

"You can't drive," he said. "You don't know how."

I had never been behind a wheel and was only fourteen, but I told him, "Yes I can."

He just threw me the keys and said, "Go ahead—drive."

I didn't know what I was supposed to do, so I got behind the wheel and asked, "How do you start it?"

"Okay, I'll start it." David put his left foot over, stepped on the gas, turned the key, and the motor started. "Now, put your foot on the brake. Bring this down to D for drive—go."

And I went. I went down the street as if I had been driving for months, to the music of Dionne Warwick playing on the 8-track. That's all David had playing in that car the whole time I was in Detroit.

"Shit, you drive good!" said David. "Slow, but good."

I drove to the store and back, and it must have taken a long time because when we came back Flo was standing out in front of the house, and as soon as we pulled up she said, "God, y'all took so *long*." And then, kind of surprised, "Tony, I didn't know you drove!"

"I don't. This was my first time."

"I thought you said you knew how to drive," David said.

"Well, I do. But my father never let me."

As I got to know David over the years, I found out that by the time *he* was fourteen, he had already been on stage for eight years singing spirituals and was ready to leave home and go out on the road. When he was in grade school he sang with Mahalia Jackson. There was a lot about his early childhood that David kept from people, but I did know that he came from a very poor family in Meridian, Mississippi, that his mother had died while he was a baby, and that he was raised by his abusive father, a hell-and-brimstone Southern preacher, his brother Jimmy and a sister, and later by a stepmother.

After he left home, David drifted. Once, when he was trying to get a job working with the horses at the New Orleans racetrack, he met a traveling minister who doubled as a pimp, "Father" Eddie Bush. Eddie Bush, who traveled in less than godly circles, took David under his wing and introduced him to a whole new life, while David drove for him, singing in bars along the way. Eddie Bush had filed adoption papers for David so he could legally travel with him. That's why David's very first solo single, before he ever joined the Tempts, was released under the name "Little Eddie Bush."

Later, in Memphis, David joined the Dixie Nightingales and traveled with them for a time doing the gospel circuit. He switched to pop when he heard Sam Cooke, then got a lesson in the star persona when he appeared on the same talent show as Elvis Presley in Arkansas. By the time he arrived in Michigan, David was still a teenager but had more behind him than all the other Tempts put together.

In fact, next to David the four other Temptations were like newborn babies. David had already been scraped hard, which was probably why he was the first Temptation to start looking at what was going on and to demand to be treated like an adult. And yet, perhaps Otis was smarter. He bided his time, asked no questions, stayed in Berry's good books, walked on good terms with Berry, and kept a firm grip on his leadership role in what had become the world's number-one black male recording group.

Chapter Two

Sit Back and Watch the Show

It was hard in late 1966 to see why David Ruffin or any other Temptation should want to complain about Motown. After all, the Tempts were way up on the A list. All through that year and the next, the Temptations were riding high on hit after hit. When, in late 1966, the group failed to make a big hit on the pop charts with Smokey's "Get Ready," featuring Eddie on lead, Motown didn't waste any time. It gave another young and hopeful writer-producer the privilege of working with the Tempts. This was Norman Whitfield, a longtime fan of the Primes who'd been waiting for just such an opportunity to show Gordy what he could do.

With the new lease on life provided by Whitfield, the Temptations were making more money than they had ever dreamed of, and they were having lots of fun spending it on homes, cars, and tons of clothes—especially Eddie. Sometimes it seemed as if Eddie wore a brand new outfit every two minutes. The Tempts were not just pop stars any more. They were becoming celebrities, TV personalities, household names. They appeared on screens all across America—on shows like "The Hollywood Palace," where Bing Crosby hosted and switched off leads on "My Girl" with David Ruffin.

In late 1966 Motown started pairing the Tempts and the Supremes on tours and television shows. Gordy called it "piggybacking." It was a smart way of gaining wider appeal for both groups. The Tempts attracted that crowd of younger, hipper people who had started to drift away from the very demure Supremes. The Supremes, on the other hand, had taken the sophisticated, white supper-club crowd by storm with their appearances at New York's Copacabana and in Las Vegas, which was exactly the direction Motown wanted to take the Tempts.

The first time the Temptations actually traded off songs with the Supremes was on "The Ed Sullivan Show" in the summer of 1967. By then "The Supremes" had become "Diana Ross and the Supremes." Between the time of the picnic and the Ed Sullivan appearance, Florence had been thrown out of the group quite brutally and out of Motown because she would not play Gordy's game—she would not accept the Supremes' name change, she would not let herself be put in the background behind Diana, she would not shut up, and Berry Gordy had heard enough of her mouth.

Although this was one of the first appearances of the new Diana Ross and the Supremes on "The Ed Sullivan Show," they arrived with a superior attitude because the group was a fixture there by now, while the Temptations were still relatively new there. On top of that, the Supremes were staying at the Hilton, while the Temptations had been booked directly across the street from them at the Warwick—which, the Tempts pointed out, was not as prestigious. But it didn't trouble them for long because they were the ones who were having all the fun.

The Supremes, on one side of the street, had their regular, well-behaved crowd around them and everything was under control. The

Temptations' scene on the other side of the street was more like a circus. They were all clowning around and had hordes of people around them, including an entourage of women who all looked like cheap versions of the Marvelettes or the Supremes, with teeny mini-skirts, patent-leather hip boots, great big earrings, and Supremes-type wigs. These women were noisy and gauche, constantly arguing with each other and pushing each other, and wherever the Tempts were, they were—in the dressing room, in the hotel lobby, in elevators, in hotel rooms.

Of course, most of these fans didn't make it past the stage door of the Ed Sullivan Theater. I'd see them there next to the Supremes fans, who were mainly young teenagers snapping pictures and asking for autographs. Those Tempts fans didn't want to hear about Diana Ross. When the Supremes came out they would just step back out of the way and give Diana a bitchy look, as if to say, She don't look all that hot—she got on the same wig as me! They were probably jealous of the Supremes, because they figured those girls could have any damn Temptation they wanted any time they wanted.

Inside the Ed Sullivan Theater it was calmer, but the mood was tense. All the Tempts had been pretty close to Flo, and had watched from a distance the brutal way in which she'd been thrown out and replaced by Cindy Birdsong—without resistance from Mary Wilson, and apparently with Diana's blessing. They had even sent Mary a telegram, telling her to "Stick by Flo." To make things worse, Diana Ross was now going around with her nose up in the air and an attitude that said, You don't have to show me where to go because this is basically my show and I know the ropes.

Meanwhile, David was unhappy with the way the set had been designed. Several boxes had been built and printed with the names "The Temptations" and "The Supremes" all across them. But if those names came up thirty times, the name "Diana Ross" came up sixty and, worst of all, her name was overlapping not just the

Supremes' name, but the Temptations' too. So, visually, you had something like, "DIANA ROSS TEMPTATIONS DIANA ROSS SUPREMES," and there was nothing the Tempts could do about it.

However, the real problem came when the two groups started rehearsing and realized that, of course, the Tempts songs and the Supremes songs were arranged in different keys, and Diana could not sing in David's key. She had a lot of trouble. David and Eddie were trying to help and encourage her, and at first she tried. But after about five minutes of them saying, "Girlfriend, you can do it. Don't worry about it," and her not hitting it quite right, she got very stubborn and adopted a Don't-tell-me-what-to-do attitude. David Ruffin, on the other hand, had no problem singing Diana's songs in her key, and neither did Eddie.

As usual, after the rehearsal Diana started complaining about the whole thing, and when the Tempts came back for rehearsal the next day they all knew she must have run and called Berry Gordy, because everything had been changed. Overnight, somebody had transposed the Tempts' charts into Diana's key and rehearsed the band to play the new charts.

The guys were shocked. They hadn't worked with Diana in a while, and they weren't used to seeing her treated almost like a solo star, with her own separate staff and everything. Little did they know that through all of this, Diana was upset because she felt the Temptations were just riding on her coattails.

"Is this what goes on all the time?" David whispered to Mary Wilson.

"Yes," said Mary, "she always gets her way."

David Ruffin was probably looking at all this and thinking, Hmm, I should be treated this way too. Just as the name of the Supremes had been changed to Diana Ross and the Supremes, he'd been thinking that the name Temptations should be changed to David Ruffin and the Temptations. Diana was the lead singer. David was the lead singer for most of the songs and as far as he was concerned he was a real singer who could sing in any key, whereas Diana's voice only sounded good when it was carefully packaged. And then you had Martha and the Vandellas, Smokey Robinson and the Miracles, Junior Walker and the All Stars. It made perfect sense to him.

When David told me about his idea after rehearsal one day he sounded quite positive that "David Ruffin and the Temptations featuring Eddie Kendrick" would be acceptable. He said he was planning to talk to Wanda Rogers about the name of her group being changed to Wanda Young and the Marvelettes so there would be some uniformity to these names. I asked him, "What about the Four Tops?" But he said they couldn't change that name because it would have to be "Levi Stubbs and the Three Tops," or else they would have to bring in an extra singer to make it four.

I was out with David on a midtown shopping expedition at the time, and I noticed that he was acting quite the star. He bought silk shirts and pants, twelve multicolored knit shirts, walking canes and a cape, sharkskin suits, a whole collection of shoes—alligator shoes, lizard shoes, green turtle shoes—and a new pair of stylish eyeglass frames. And he didn't stop there—he bought me six new outfits too. David had become a flamboyant spender.

Later, before the show, David told me, "Watch, Tony. When I get up there tonight, I'm gonna give that phony, wig-wearin' bitch a run for her money." I didn't know what he was planning, but I knew David could murder Diana vocally, and he did. He did exactly what he was supposed to do as far as his dance steps and movements were concerned. But when it came to singing, he did a whole lot of ad libbing and completely threw Diana off.

David was the kind of performer who could create a show of his own in five minutes, whereas Diana had to be highly rehearsed. She didn't have that flexibility and David knew it. Besides, he could sing much louder than Diana, which meant that she had to really strain her voice to keep up. Diana came across sounding squeaky and whiny, and needless to say she was livid by the end of it.

Nevertheless, the show was a huge success and the Temptations went on to do several more paired appearances and albums with Diana Ross and the Supremes, including Motown's first television special, "TCB," in 1969, and the less successful, Diana-dominated "GIT on Broadway" that followed. But by that time David Ruffin was long gone.

David had been quickly making enemies at Motown. His suggestion that the Temptations' name be changed to reflect his lead position created a furor both within and outside the group—Eddie didn't like the idea one bit. As he said, why not have it changed to "Eddie Kendrick and the Temptations"? Otis just tossed out the idea as if it was a total absurdity.

The whole name issue also added to David's growing reputation as an egomaniac. When he bought himself a limo of his own so he didn't have to ride with the rest of the group, and insisted on showing up in cowboy boots and a cowboy hat when everyone else was in tuxedos, he only brought more hard feelings upon himself. People closest to David, however, saw his actions not so much as a sign of an over-inflated ego, but more as an index of his struggle to maintain his own individual identity. He'd tell me about how hard it was for an entertainer to be considered a person rather than merely an object.

As time went by all of the Temptations' egos grew fast, which wasn't surprising given that each had his own little army of ass-kissers running behind him and telling him he was a star, and of course each had his wife or lover or buddy telling him, "Honey, you should get more to do. Darling, it isn't fair. Why's David doing all that? Why did Eddie get that lead? Why don't they give you more?"

They all had their fans and followers, but David's were the ones that Motown really objected to. Eddie was always very careful not to publicly associate with people who were outwardly questionable, but David hung out with whomever he felt like hanging out with, and they were not people that Motown wanted around their stars— people like Eddie Bush, and a handsome hanger-on named Royce who spent most of his time trying to talk David up into the biggest star you could ever imagine.

There was another problem. While several performers at Motown experimented with drugs during the late sixties, and many more drank, David was quickly turning into a hard-core user. He had started with marijuana and alcohol—it was rare to see him go on stage without first downing half a tumbler of gin and soda. Now he was into snorting cocaine and taking pills too. The alcohol got him on stage, the coke kept the excitement level up after the perfor- mance, and the pills helped him wind down when, finally, he wanted to get some sleep. The result of all these drugs, put together with David's feeling that he was irreplaceable, was that he started showing up late, missing performances, and generally acting like a superstar instead of a "team player," as Otis put it.

At the same time, David had started making louder and louder noises about Motown—not that he was the only one who questioned Motown's finances. Many Motown artists had woken up when they saw what happened to Flo Ballard and how, despite so many million- selling records, she did not leave with her pockets lined. Besides, by late 1967 Motown had become a very different place. Instead of being a familylike organization where everybody shared a passion for music and nobody cared if they had to paint walls or help out by doing background vocals, it had become a large corporation headed predominantly by hard-nosed white executives who had very little feel for or interest in the music, and didn't care who had helped out in the old days—the bottom line was the bottom line.

So there was not much love lost between the artists and Motown. But David was the only one, apart from Martha Reeves, who came out openly against the company and not only battled against the paternalistic system but also questioned its credibility. When the group met in private you'd hear Eddie saying things like, "My real daddy wouldn't do me like this," and they'd all dog Big Daddy Gordy. When they all met with Gordy and David spoke up, however, none of the others would support him. Perhaps they didn't approve of David's point-blank style. Never subtle, he would think nothing of shouting "Where's our goddamn money, motherfucker?" directly in Gordy's face.

According to David, that's when Motown began to campaign openly against him. At first, the campaign centered around David's apparent ego problems and his live-in relationship with Tammi Terrell, a beautiful young girl who had come to Motown in 1965 after an unsuccessful and harrowing stint as a background singer with James Brown's revue. Tammi was something of a tarnished angel when the company first signed her—a promiscuous alcoholic who, it was said, had had a tempestuous relationship with James Brown. Motown sent her first to the company dentist to fix up her teeth, and then straight to Artist Development, where her rough edges were smoothed out and her reputation smoothed over.

Before you knew it, Tammi was Motown's golden girl who could do no wrong. In 1966 she was paired with Marvin Gaye, and by the end of 1967 they were an established duo, with two big hits to their name. Berry knew a money-maker when he saw one. It was in Motown's interests to keep Tammi clean and working. It's possible that the company also wanted to encourage the public's assumption that Marvin and Tammi, whose duets were intensely romantic, were lovers—despite a very jealous Anna Gordy Gaye.

Meanwhile, the relationship between David and Tammi had grown mutually destructive and openly tempestuous, though no less close. They fought, they made up, they drank, they slept around. I remember going shopping with Tammi one time when she told me a story about how she discovered David fooling around with someone else, and to spite him went and jumped right into bed with Eddie Kendrick. Seeing Tammi with black eyes and bruises, people at Motown started telling each other that she was a good girl who deserved somebody better than David Ruffin—of course, all the men would have preferred to have Tammi for themselves. Then, all of a sudden, in the summer of '67 Tammi collapsed on stage midway through a performance with Marvin. She was rushed to the hospital and diagnosed as having a brain tumor.

Immediately, the rumors started to fly. People said that Tammi's tumor was a result of David having beaten her up, of David having hit her over the head with a bar stool or a hammer—the details varied, but the rumors hurt David badly. In fact, Tammi had apparently suffered beatings at the hands of at least a couple of other people, both in and out of Motown. Over the next couple of years until her death in 1970, Tammi was in and out of the hospital for one operation after another. She was never the same again, nor was David. Marvin Gaye was so upset that he practically stopped working for three years.

In 1967 Motown moved its center of operations from the old Hitsville, U.S.A., to a new, impersonal office building where the artists could no longer feel comfortable coming and going and hanging out. The family spirit had completely faded, along with Berry Gordy's image as the beneficent father. At times, it even seemed as if Gordy was no longer actively involved in the creative end of things at Motown. While Ralph Seltzer, a white attorney, took over the creative division, Berry spent more and more time in Los Angeles, where he was getting ready to launch Diana Ross's big movie career. Absolutely everything now centered around Diana, much to the displeasure of the other artists.

Nevertheless, when Otis Williams cited Berry Gordy's "No one person is greater than the group" as the reason that Ruffin should be ousted from the Tempts, nobody pointed to the obvious—nobody said, "What about Diana Ross and what about the Supremes?" David's image was so tainted by now that nobody cared. He had been acting arrogant and irresponsible, and when he failed to show up for an important engagement because he preferred to keep a date with Dean Martin's daughter, the group felt that he had gone too far.

A meeting was called in David's absence, and the decision was taken to fire him. Motown, presumably, was in full agreement. I never knew how Eddie felt about it, but in similar situations I've heard him say, basically, "I'm not going to wear myself out. I'm not going to think about it. You do what you can do about a situation, put your trust in God, then sit back and watch the show." Anyway, Eddie probably had no choice. Without David there, Otis and Melvin would surely get their way.

Of course, David had been asking for it—in a sense, he fired himself. He'd been talking about going solo, but doing it in such a way that he could still be a member of the Temptations. He wanted change, but he didn't really want to leave. I don't believe that he ever imagined he would be fired, because by now David thought he *was* the Temptations. Of course, he knew what had happened to Flo—he was helping and supporting her during the tough times she was having, and even compared himself to her: "She's a no-nonsense person, like me. She don't take no shit," he'd tell me. But, unlike Flo Ballard, David was a lead singer, the voice of the Temptations. How could they fire him? In early summer of 1968 David was called into an executive meeting at Motown, where he was informed that he was out of the group and still under contract to the company. He could hardly believe it. But when he went to the Temptations performance that night he found a new lead singer there, Dennis Edwards, who had been secretly rehearsing with the group for two weeks.

Over the next few years, David would try again and again to be accepted as a Temptation once more, to no avail. He desperately missed the roar of the crowd, the spotlights, the road, the calamity. He probably even missed the group. He would come to a show and sit desolately in the audience until it seemed like the right time for him to leap up on the stage, grab a mike, and sing like he'd sung that first time with the Tempts in a little club in Michigan. After David had been dragged offstage on a couple of occasions, Motown hired special security people for the Temptations' shows and David was refused admittance.

Although David had been informed that he remained under contract to Motown, he characterized that contract as "one-sided," and immediately signed with another management company and a separate booking agency, who offered him no end of engagements and also put his name forward for parts in two movies. David had always wanted to act—he thought he'd be perfect as a cowboy or a minister. Motown immediately sued him for breach of contract, forcing him to return to the company, where he had to wait a full year before recording his first solo, "My Whole World Ended (the Moment You Left Me)."

The record was a hit, and for a short time David enjoyed a successful solo career. He told the press that he still missed the Tempts, but "if you put on a new shoe and you wear it as long as you wore the old shoe you took off, I think you become comfortable"—David was crazy about shoes, and he had a fabulous way with words. He said that at first he would be on stage by himself and, forgetting, make a move into the background to join the others, only to discover that there was no background and there were no others. But, he said, as time went by he found that being solo just meant there was more room to move.

Although both of David's 1969 releases—"My Whole World" and "I Lost Everything I Love"—were hits, that was it for him until his 1975 comeback song, "Walk Away from Love." For seven years he was put on the back burner and held there. By 1970 the great David Ruffin had been reduced to doing occasional performances

in second-rate clubs. It was an impossible situation, both emotionally and financially debilitating. David called it "economic peon-
age," and he would never forgive Motown for it.

The Temptations, meanwhile, were flying. With Dennis Edwards's deep and gutsy lead voice, they recorded Whitfield's "Cloud
Nine" in late 1968 and set the tone for a whole new kind of Motown
sound—the driving, progressive sound of their later hits like "Psy-
chedelic Shack" and "Papa Was a Rolling Stone." Just as unusual
were the song's lyrics, about the joys of getting high. Of course, at
the time Berry Gordy denied that the song had anything to do with
drugs. But years later he would admit to having known what the
subject of the song was, and to having ignored it because he knew
it was going to be a hit. Otis, however, was still towing the line,
claiming that the song was simply about having a good attitude.

With "Cloud Nine," which reached number six on the charts
and got the group their first Grammy, the public enthusiastically
accepted Dennis into the Temptations. But within the group itself
Dennis had a much harder time, despite the fact that Otis and Eddie
had personally picked him as David's replacement, and the others
had agreed. He was and would always remain an outsider among
the Temptations.

I always wondered if things might have been better for Dennis
if he hadn't been so diffident. "I'm not the lead singer of the Temptations," he'd say, "I'm a Temptation." Dennis had been a big
Temptations fan, and above all a David Ruffin fan, from the time
he'd heard "My Girl" on the radio while he was in the army. When
he came to Motown as a session pianist, and later as a fill-in singer
with the Contours, his dream was to sing with the Tempts. By the
time his dream had come true, he realized it wasn't enough to have
a great voice. He felt that he couldn't rival David. Though he had
a raw appeal, he didn't have the mystique or the energy. When he
tried throwing his mike up in the air and catching it the way David

did, he just dropped it. It was hard enough trying to learn the intricate dance steps and keep in time with the movements.

The Temptations continued to put out hit after hit, and the money kept on rolling in, and Dennis Edwards started looking like a real star with a new gold bracelet on his wrist one day and his name spelled on it in diamonds the next. But the Temptations were slowly falling apart. Paul Williams had been hitting the bottle more and more, as well as partying more and more, and by 1969 he was fucking up dance steps, missing lyrics, and sweating profusely. Eventually, a singer named Richard Street—one of the original Distants who'd been eased out to make room for Eddie and Paul, and now a member of Motown's Quality Control department—was brought out to stand in the wings and sing Paul's parts while Paul tried to keep himself together on stage.

Eddie was having problems too. Having expected to become the dominant lead when David left the group, he found that he was more in the background than ever, because Norman Whitfield relied almost exclusively on Dennis's voice. At the same time, Dennis left Eddie plenty of room to become the superstar personality of the group, and his ego grew proportionately. Along with that, he developed a new bitterness against Motown and against anyone who seemed to be in Motown's pocket—especially Otis.

Eddie wasn't the only one who was growing more bitter by the day. Quite a few Motown artists were rallying against the company. Even the songwriters and producers were disgruntled—including the irreplaceable team of Holland-Dozier-Holland, who left Motown in 1968 because Berry refused to split publishing royalties with them. When Motown sued for breach of contract, H-D-H countersued the company for conspiracy, fraud, and deceit. They later charged that, as a result of the suit, Motown had harassed, intimidated, and blacklisted them. Because the parties settled out of court, I don't know who had to pay whom.

This was no longer a happy family. In the early days everybody had been happy to work for practically nothing because they felt they all had a stake in the company, and the better Motown did, the better they would do. Now the company was making millions, but the artists' contracts still offered the same one-sided conditions and pitiful royalties, way below industry standards. Several of the artists, including Marvin Gaye, were also fighting Motown to let them write and produce some of their own material, an idea that the company resisted with all its might until finally, in 1971, Marvin Gaye was allowed to produce *What's Going On*, an album Gordy hated and almost refused to release. Of course it is now considered one of the greatest albums of all time.

When a group of Motown artists and producers decided to call a meeting to discuss negotiating tactics, Motown sent some guys to sit outside in a car and report on who attended. Surveillance was nothing new at Motown—even in the early days some of the valets or the road managers would be paid to report on who slept with whom, who was seen going into whose room late at night, and so on. Berry always needed to know exactly what was going on. In the early days he even used to use me as an unwitting spy. He'd ask me things like, "Tony, did you go back to the hotel with the Tempts?"

I'd say, "Yes, Mr. Gordy."

"Whose room did you go to? Oh, you were hanging out with Eddie. I guess he had a big crowd up there, huh?"

"No, he didn't have anybody up there."

"Nobody? Are you sure? Because I know a lot of people like to follow Eddie."

"Well, only so-and-so was there."

"Oh, she was there? What did she have on? Oh, she just had her robe on?"

It took me a while to realize what Berry was up to during those conversations. In the beginning I was just thrilled that this important man wanted to hold a conversation with me. But all that had changed by now. The whole thing was on a completely different level.

A few artists contacted David during their period of disillusionment, including Eddie Kendrick, who seemed to feel even closer to David once David was out of the group. "I told him so," David would say of Eddie's calls. "Now it's getting to him. Now the motherfucker's beginning to see. I told him so. They thought I was crazy, but they're seeing it too."

Finally, during a Temptations meeting, Eddie suggested a strike against the company. Otis dismissed the idea outright. By now, Eddie was sick and tired of the whole group mentality. He was sick of Otis and his common-sense, Let's-bite-our-tongues-and-kiss-Berry's-ass approach. He had never gotten along with Melvin, and Paul was on his way out. Dennis, whom Eddie had looked to as a potential ally now that David was gone, always seemed to side with Otis or remain neutral because that was the way to stay alive—as Eddie said, "Anywhere you want to put Dennis, you can take Dennis. He has no mind of his own."

Toward the end of 1970 it was announced that Eddie Kendrick would be going solo. He and Otis were practically at each other's throats. Eddie wanted out, Otis wanted him out, and Motown was more than willing to oblige because Dennis could carry the Tempts, and Eddie was enough of a star to carry himself—that made two money-makers out of one. In the spring of '71, as one of the Tempts' biggest hits, "Just My Imagination (Running Away with Me)," came out with Eddie singing lead, he was initially replaced by Richard Owens, and then shortly thereafter by Damon Harris, a twenty-year-old singer who sounded surprisingly like Eddie—much to Eddie's consternation. Damon quickly started questioning the way things were run in the group, and wanted Dennis to question them too. Dennis declined. That, he explained, was just the way things were, and there wasn't anything anyone could do about it.

With Eddie out of the group, Paul completely lost his balance and couldn't even fake it on stage any more. Richard Street was brought in as his replacement and Paul, still under contract, was kept on salary by Motown as a "consultant" to the Tempts.

One day in August 1973, Paul came home from work to find his girlfriend, Winnie, partying with friends. Upset, he promptly left again. He was found some time later, dead with a bullet in his brain. The verdict was suicide. Everybody agreed that Paul had plenty of reasons to kill himself—he owed eighty thousand dollars in back taxes, his family life was in ruins, a boutique he had opened with Winnie had failed, he'd drunk himself out of the Temptations, and now considered himself a prisoner of Motown. But hardly anybody really believed that Paul had killed himself.

Eddie certainly had his doubts. He had seen Paul just a couple of days earlier and had found him to be in a relatively positive mood. Besides, as David said, why would anyone get into his car with only his underwear on, drive to within a few blocks of Motown and, using his right hand, shoot himself in the *left* side of his head? It didn't make sense. Naturally the rumors flew once again. Did Paul have something on somebody? Was he threatening to run and tell? Nobody will ever know.

Whatever the reason for Paul's death, it terrified Eddie. He and Paul had come north together, and they were supposed to be successful together. Eddie could see what drugs, alcohol, and women had done to their plans. Always a religious person, Eddie became doubly so and resolved never, ever to let any of those evils interfere with his career—never to get so emotionally involved with a woman, or to get so hooked on a drug, that he would allow himself to fall. As the years went by, he became increasingly self-controlled and cautious, carefully picking and choosing who he would allow into his life.

Paul's fate also made Eddie even more wary of Motown, despite the fact that his solo career was going very well—in fact, Eddie was, alongside Stevie Wonder and Marvin Gaye, one of the most successful male solo stars at Motown during the seventies, with hits like "Keep On Truckin'" and "Boogie Down." But as well as he was doing, he was not doing as well as he thought he ought to be. Eddie thought he was going to be the male Diana Ross, but nobody could be because Gordy wouldn't let them. And nobody was given the kind of star treatment or attention she got either, which Eddie resented.

Besides, as well as Eddie was doing he could see what had happened to people like Flo Ballard, who by the mid-seventies was on welfare and still embroiled in lawsuits with Motown; or Martha Reeves, who, after being on the back burner since 1967 and suffering a series of nervous breakdowns that put her in a straitjacket for a time, was finally released by Motown in 1972. They had all been huge stars, and they were all now broke.

Eddie could also see what was happening to David, who was still struggling against Motown. "Them people," David said, "will never leave you the fuck alone. They'll find a way to get you. They'll fire you and hold you to your contract, and if your contract says you've got to do two albums a year, they'll take you to the studio and record you two times a year, and then not release the albums."

In the end, Eddie found out exactly what David was talking about. He and Berry argued over a cover for Eddie's album, *He's a Friend*—Berry, still trying to perpetuate Motown's ultra-wholesome, Middle America image, thought the way the two clasped male hands were shot had homosexual overtones. Eddie liked it and fought for it. In the end Berry let it go. He simply failed to promote the album and took note that the former Temptation was getting hard to handle.

Another time, Eddie and Gordy were in an elevator together and Gordy told Eddie, "You know, your career would go much further if you would be like Diana and just do what you're told."

"Well, I'm not Diana," Eddie replied, as the elevator doors opened and he got out.

From that point on, according to Eddie, it was as if he didn't exist at Motown. Berry just washed his hands of Eddie Kendrick.

What happened next remains something of a mystery to me. According to Eddie, he wanted out and Motown wouldn't let him go. Eddie offered to buy his way out; Motown wanted him to also sign an agreement relinquishing all future royalties. Things got so bad, Eddie said, that at one point the company had him up in a hospital seeing psychiatrists. I assume that's when Eddie signed the agreement, but Eddie would never say—even after he left Motown in 1978. If there was something he wanted you to know, he'd tell you. But if you wanted to know more, he'd just clam up. After ten years with Motown he didn't trust anyone anymore.

By 1972 Motown had relocated again, this time to Los Angeles, where they were obviously more interested in pursuing movie and television possibilities than in keeping the Sound of Young America alive. Maybe Berry thought he'd taken it as far as he could go. Times were changing, sales were dropping—Motown only had four singles in the top ten that year—he had ridden the crest of a wave and was running dry.

Almost everybody who was left packed up and moved west. Dennis took to the idea like a duck to water and immediately got himself a fab bachelor pad in Beverly Hills. Eddie, still a homeboy, didn't want to move but was forced to. He and Pat had split up and gotten back together and split up many times, but now they had split up for good. Otis and Melvin moved their wives and kids out and learned to play golf. David got left behind in Detroit.

That was when I started to hear stories circulating about Motown and the mob. The stories, none of which were ever proved to be true, were always the same: Motown got too big and the mob just knocked on the door and said, Hello, you're too big, you've got too many stars, you're on TV all the time, we want a piece of the action.

We want half of everything you take. Berry, of course, refused. He ended up in the hospital with a broken leg—or two broken legs, depending on who was telling it—after being jumped in an alley. Berry Gordy suddenly moved to L.A., although he'd been telling everyone that Motown would never leave Detroit. After all, Detroit was where he was known and respected. In later years, Eddie would often refer to the mob when he talked about Motown and about the escalation of white executives into the company, just as Mary Wilson would refer to "underworld figures."

All that was left of the original Temptations now was Otis and Melvin, both of whom were getting increasingly jealous over the fact that Dennis was getting all the attention and all the leads. On some recordings Whitfield didn't even use the other four Tempts' voices anymore; he used backup singers instead. Dennis kept telling the others he couldn't help it—it was the producer's decision.

At this point, Dennis's was the only strong voice in the group he had once practically worshipped. After David had left, he'd considered Eddie the most important Temptation. When Eddie and then Paul left, he himself thought of leaving. He held on even though he felt his opinion never counted in the group, even though his bad feelings were only getting worse, and even though he couldn't stand to hear Otis still insisting that the Tempts were the number-one male group in the world. They were clearly now on Motown's B list. Even Norman Whitfield seemed to have lost interest in the group and left in 1975 for the same reasons that so many of Motown's most talented songwriters and producers had left—money and control.

In 1976 the Tempts left Motown and moved to Atlantic Records after a legal battle over money and control of the group name. Then Dennis made the big move to go solo—only to find himself battling with Motown. The company refused to release him from his contract, even though they didn't like his first solo album and planned not to promote it, despite the fact that the album had been under their strict creative control all along.

So there were now three unhappy ex-lead singers of the Temptations—all superstars once, all solo, all unpromoted. You had five not-so-temptin' Temptations being held together as an "institution" by the two original background singers. And you had one ex-Temptation dead from a bullet in his brain. It was the end of an era—an era that started with the Temptations in their limos and their top hats and canes, with top-ten hits and roaring crowds, and that ended in half-empty concert halls, and with records that hardly anybody even noticed.

Chapter Three

I Am Still a Star!

When Berry Gordy, Jr., sold Motown Records in early 1988 it didn't seem like any big deal to me. I figured he had earned his retirement, and was just cashing out. Since the beginning of the decade, nobody I knew had been paying much attention to Motown Records. Even Diana Ross had stormed out of the company in 1981, reportedly because Gordy wouldn't honor her three conditions for re-signing: make me a vice president like Smokey; give me my own label, Ross Records; and most important of all, finally make me Mrs. Gordy.

Diana had been watching her friend Cher take charge of her own life and career, and she wanted to do the same. She was sick of being dependent on a man with a cigar. According to the grapevine, Diana told Berry that she would quit if he didn't give her what she wanted, and he said, No way. He didn't believe she'd do it. No one believed Ross would leave the cocoon Berry had sheltered her in. Nevertheless, she said good-bye. That's when she discovered that the yellow convertible Rolls-Royce and the super-stretch Mercedes that Gordy had had gift-wrapped and delivered to her door as birthday and Christmas presents had never really been hers. They were just perks of her employment at Motown, owned by the company, little extras that Gordy sent someone to retrieve when Diana, no longer an employee, had stopped playing the game.

Gordy had changed very little, but Motown had. By the 1980s, it was a completely different company from the one that a bunch of struggling musicians had helped build. The Sound of Young America had become the sound of aging America, the sound of a generation trying to relive its youth. Motown, reported to be even then among the biggest black-owned companies in America, was keeping busy living very comfortably off its past.

Berry was still living in his multimillion-dollar, Tudor-style, Bel Air mansion, surrounded by ten acres of private land, tons of bodyguards, and a massive security system. Gordy was chairman of the company now—which meant that he often didn't leave the safety of his mansion for months on end, and when he did it was to sweep into the office and rearrange the staff, demoting and promoting as the fancy took him. In 1983 he presided over Motown's birthday celebration telecast, "Motown 25." It was the biggest thing Motown had done in years, and although the show was subtitled "Yesterday, Today, and Tomorrow," it was really about yesterday.

Most of the stars who were invited to perform at "Motown 25" were only back home for the evening, seemingly happy to pay tribute to the family that had molded them. They, like Motown itself, had been living in a kind of shadow land of yesterday, roaming the world performing the same old hits that gave us all butterflies once—and sometimes still did. But, unlike Gordy, most of them were not ensconced in any mansions. Like people displaced by an earthquake or war, many of them were living on the edge financially and emotionally, trying to put their lives back together in the image of the lives they had once known.

I was working as road manager and jack-of-all-trades for Mary Wilson now that she had left the Supremes and gone out as a solo act with her own fake "Supremes" background singers. Times had been tough for Mary. Long gone was the impressive mansion in Los Angeles' exclusive Hancock Park area. She was now down on her luck, divorced from her abusive husband, and living near L.A. in the Valley, with her four children, mother, and cousin in a tiny, two-bedroom bungalow in Studio City—suffering from the scars of being a former Supreme discovered singing old hits and squeezing into old gowns.

With bookings so few and far between, working for Mary was more of a hobby for me, something I'd been doing since I met the Supremes and started running errands for them. And just like some people start collecting stamps when they're kids and never stop collecting, even when they become bank managers or electricians, I carried on doing this work even after I'd embarked on a lucrative career selling real estate on Long Island. I did it because I loved Mary like a sister, and hoped that she would succeed. Besides, it was fun, it was adventure, it was comical, it was sometimes limos at the curb and first-class hotel rooms. It was going somewhere and having a fuss made over you because you were working for a Supreme or a Temptation. It was a good life, and nothing was more tempting.

I could only guess that Mary, and other ex-Motowners we would meet on the road from time to time, kept going for the same kinds of reasons that I did. How else could they have kept on being stars? They'd lived this life since they were teenagers, and if people still wanted to hear those old hits, they were ready to keep on singing them, even if it seemed like it was all downhill. Besides, they loved to perform in front of a live audience. They loved the people—live people with warm hands clapping for them, appreciating them. This gave validity to who they were and who they once had been. It told them, "I am still a star, and I will live each and every moment as a star."

And then there were the fans who would come backstage after the shows. They'd bring their kids, who were now eighteen or twenty years old. They'd push the kid forward: "This is my daughter. She was conceived to 'Get Ready.' " The kid would be embarrassed, but the parents would think it was wonderful that these people were still singing. The fans just loved the fact that they could come to a concert and hear the music that made them feel young again, that reminded them of a happier time, of the sixties, of life before the Vietnam War and before kids and mortgages, fat and gray hair. So the fans loved them, fussed over them. And the performers ate it up.

Mary Wells was in even worse shape than Mary Wilson. Having been involved at different times with two of the Womack brothers, she was now still living with one of them, who not only managed her but also sang with her. Mary was touring as a nostalgia act with her baby daughter in tow, taking on just enough work to feed herself and her children, while quietly suffering the physical and mental abuses of her lover.

We would see her on the road from to time, nursing a black eye or a bruise. One night, in Westbury, Long Island, after an argument about money, Mr. Womack went really crazy. He started by cutting up Mary's Louis Vuitton suitcases. Then he threw everything she owned out the window into the parking lot, which had just been covered in fresh, wet, black asphalt, took her money, and left her on the road with her baby, Sugar. I had to go to the local mall the next morning and pick out a dress for her to wear and some cosmetics for that evening's show, because she had absolutely nothing. But the fans didn't know it. They loved her for who she had been in their lives, and as long as she sang "My Guy" and "Two Lovers" they didn't care that she was now an overweight platinum blonde who was singing for her survival.

Martha Reeves was touring alone without any staff or entourage because she was trying to economize—unlike some ex-Motown stars, she was always realistic. She had trained countless groups of Vandellas in cities all around the globe so that she could save money on hotel bills and travel.

Martha wasn't as caught up in that Forever-a-Star syndrome as Mary Wilson the Supreme. But she was still under the spell of the competitive spirit fostered at Motown, and she was still looking for that nod of acknowledgment from her old boss, Berry Gordy—and would keep on looking until she got it in 1991, when Gordy finally called her to settle a suit she had brought against him because he had allegedly ripped her off on royalties from her 1963 hit, "Heat Wave." After half a lifetime of bitterness and a two-year legal battle, all he had to do was call and say, Hi Martha, sorry it went so far, I'll give you your money, I'll always take care of you. One fatherly pat on the head, and all that bitterness was wiped away. "No hard feelings," Martha told him. She was back in the fold, back in his arms again.

Martha had her fake Vandellas and Mary Wilson had her fake Supremes, but the Marvelettes, whose name like so many others had been retained by Motown, were completely fake. The group was now a second-generation phenomena managed by a white promoter who had apparently won the name from Gordy at a gambling table, and who was now cleaning up by keeping various groups of very young Marvelettes running around the globe recreating the classic songs, one group appearing in London, say, while the other performed in New York.

Marvin Gaye, meanwhile, was living in self-imposed exile in Europe. He had hit rock bottom after his emotionally and financially debilitating divorce from Anna Gordy—a divorce that resulted in a court-ordered double album whose earnings went directly to Marvin's ex-wife, who was also his boss's sister. The album, *Here, My Dear*, was Marvin's way of paying Anna back in hate and humiliation what the court had intended him to pay back in money, and he knew all along that Gordy was going to have to release it even though he would be releasing an album that trashed his own sister. After the album, Marvin had run first to Hawaii and then all the way to Europe to escape the clutches of not only Motown and the entire Gordy clan, but also of various creditors including the IRS, to whom he owed untold thousands in back taxes.

Mary Wilson and I visited Marvin in London one time when we were there on tour, because Mary was looking to get herself a recording contract by having Marvin produce an album for her. Never one to mince words, she spent the whole day talking to a very high Marvin about nothing but this album that she wanted to do with him, and when he played a cassette of some tracks he was working on with Harvey Fuqua—what was to become the *Midnight Love* album—she insisted on trying to sing along with him. High herself, she was completely out of key. I couldn't bear it.

When Mary left to go home to the States, Marvin asked me if I could stay on for a week or so and help him out with a few things. That's when I discovered that Marvin Gaye liked to dress in drag.

"Who did Mary's hair?" Marvin asked me almost as soon as Mary was gone.

"Honey, I threw that wig together for her," I told him. "I hate to take credit for it because it's so hard to work on synthetic hair, I can never get it to look quite right."

"Do you think you could do my hair?"

"Well, your hair's very short, Marvin. There's not much we could do with that."

"No, I meant a wig!"

I thought he was going to put on a toupee, but he meant a wig. He liked the experience of having a woman's wig on his head, all rolled up—but he didn't want it styled on a wig head, he wanted me to roll it on him, like he was in a beauty shop and this was his own hair. Some days I would do two or three styles for him! Then he would get himself dressed up. Marvin had found a nice selection of clothes over there in the cross-dressing shops. He had the cross-sex undergarments and everything. He wasn't that interested in makeup. What he really liked were the bras, corsets, garter belts, and negligees that he would wear around the apartment with nothing else on top—just a wig on his head with rollers in it like any old housewife. Later, when Marvin's father shot him dead in 1984 and the whole story of their troubled relationship came out, I discovered that the Reverend Gay was into wigs too.

Still, although Marvin looked kind of funny in a wig and a beard, it wasn't the way he dressed that made me think he was weird. It was more the way he would just sit and gaze out of the huge windows he had in his apartment. Although he was talking to me, he seemed to be in a conversation all of his own. Everything he said sounded like it had this greater spiritual meaning, but I thought it was really a lot of bullshit, an excuse for being high and talking at the same time. I thought it was really all too much and a little crazy.

One of the only Motown groups that didn't seem to have any scandal or controversy connected to them was the Four Tops, who had left the company in 1972 and returned again in 1983. They were still together after thirty years, still sane, still in demand.

The Tempts, as always under the firm grip of Otis Williams, who was still insisting that he was their founder and only legitimate spokesman, had returned to the Motown family in 1980 when they decided that leaving home wasn't such a good idea after all. The group was a true revolving door, with singers constantly coming and going and coming back again, and Otis still chastising them when they were bad. The way I saw it, that was Otis's way of staying alive. He had to keep the whole Temptations thing under strict control, because if it fell apart he'd have nothing left. Unlike Melvin, whose *basso profundo* got him quite a bit of session work, Otis didn't have any real voice or name of his own. His claim to fame lies buried in the name The Temptations.

Dennis Edwards had come back to the group in 1980 after things didn't work out with his replacement, Louis Price. Otis warned him that they would not "tolerate any nonsense." With Dennis back, and the nostalgia boom kicking in, Motown decided to engineer a Temptations reunion album and tour in 1982, bringing Eddie Kendrick and David Ruffin back together with Otis and Melvin. Dennis Edwards made five, and for some reason Richard Street and Glenn Leonard were kept on with the group, despite the fact that Otis had been threatening to throw Glenn out for repeated drunkenness. All of a sudden there were seven Temptations. But who was counting?

Neither Eddie nor David had been working much since the collapse of their solo careers. In 1981 Eddie had moved from Arista to Atlantic, without much success. The Tempts hadn't been doing all that well either—which was the only reason why I could see that any of them agreed to the reunion. The former Primes and former Distants had scarcely spoken to each other since Paul Williams's funeral in 1973 and they probably would have preferred it that way, but hey—why not put all that aside and cash in on the past? Maybe it would even work out as a permanent, profitable idea. Eddie, following his own reasoning that "if you don't use your God-given talent you're gonna lose it," had been taking whatever jobs came up, which didn't amount to much because the word was out that Eddie Kendrick had already lost it. David Ruffin, meanwhile, had been in and out of trouble as usual. As the tour began in the spring of 1982, he was wanted by the IRS for failure to pay fifty thousand dollars in 1976 federal taxes.

The tour was tightly scheduled and exhausting. For seven or eight months they seemed to be always moving from one place to another, playing classic Tempts material to sold-out crowds. David, of course, was the star of the show, over forty but still doing those spins and splits as if it was the most natural thing in the world. And for him it was. Predictably, there was a lot of tension out on the road. David discovered a drug buddy in Dennis Edwards. Now, having resisted freebasing cocaine for some time because he knew that once he started he wouldn't be able to stop, he discovered the pipe—which didn't do his asthma much good.

The *Reunion* album was recorded featuring all seven Temptations, with David's lead vocal on one track and Dennis's on all the others. During this time, David had also been approached by Motown with a proposition he couldn't refuse: go into the studio and cut an album, and the company would take care of his tax problem. David flew to California, started work in the studio with producer George Tobin, and apparently spent the next few days in the luxury hotel room they had booked him, smoking his way through the few-thousand-dollar advance he had been given, and refusing to come out. After cutting a couple of outstanding tracks between hotel-room stints, David returned to Detroit. When Motown called to try to set up studio time, David refused. Privately, he complained that they wanted him to do everything over and over again although he felt he didn't need to, and that the whole thing was too rushed, too strenuous. According to friends, David was figuring on returning to L.A. and finishing the album in November, when the reunion tour was due to end.

By the time the reunion tour did finally finish—after the only-to-be-expected fights about control, after Eddie and David had stalked out of one meeting at Motown saying that they refused to be treated like kids anymore, and after David and Dennis had both spent much of their money and time getting high—by then it was too late for David. He had a date for sentencing in court.

Nevertheless, David didn't seem too concerned about his tax problems. He went to court acting as if it was all taken care of, and came out screaming, "They're not gonna do this to me again!" David had been counting on Motown. But Gordy's ex-wife, Raynoma, had basically accepted this project as a dare in her ongoing battle of wits with Berry. The way she saw it, it was Gordy saying, bet you can't tame Ruffin. The end result was that David was hit with a five-thousand-dollar fine and sentenced to spend six months and a day in federal prison camp in Indiana. Right after that, David received a letter from Motown informing him that the company did not wish to exercise its option to extend its agreement. "We wish you continued success, Very truly yours . . ." David felt as if Motown had kept the IRS off his back until the tour was over and the record wasn't happening, and then said, "We have no use for you."

When David finally got adjusted to being in jail, he made sure he got himself a job in the greenhouse where it was warm and he could pass his days watering the plants and taking naps. The rest of the time he reflected on his life, made several beautiful clocks from pieces of wood in the arts and crafts workshop, and put on some shows. He also read his Bible diligently, looking for justice and reason and deliverance from temptation. After four months and a day he was allowed to go home.

The only problem was that David no longer had a home. While he had been in jail his beautiful house had been foreclosed by the bank and put up for sale. David's brother, Jimmy, and his girlfriend, Debbie, had managed to salvage a few of his belongings and move them into storage for him. That was all he had left. David moved onto the farm that Debbie was managing and spent the next two years mending fences, working with livestock, training horses, and trying to stay away from drugs and everything that he associated with drugs. He listened to tapes that Bobby Womack and other friends sent him of their unreleased material, and once in a while he could be heard singing along. Then you'd hear him humming pieces of his own tunes, trying to come up with lyrics.

Eddie went back to obscurity too, while Otis and his Tempts, who replaced Glenn Leonard's Kendrick-like tenor with Ron Tyson's Kendrick-like tenor right after the reunion tour, treaded water for a while until Motown came up with another blast-from-the-past idea. They took the Tempts and the Four Tops, who had just returned to Motown after a surprisingly successful ten-year stint at ABC, teamed the Tempts back up with Norman Whitfield and the Tops with the songwriters who had made their dreams come true, Holland-Dozier-Holland, put the two groups in adjoining studios, and had them cut competing albums.

It was the old formula again, including a classic duel of the voices between Tempts' lead singer Dennis Edwards and Tops' lead singer Levi Stubbs. Then they sent them out together on a "T 'n' T" tour, but failed to promote the albums effectively. At the end of the tour, Otis decided that Dennis Edwards was still not playing the game properly and decided to replace him with a young singer by the name of Ollie Woodson—a singer they had considered hiring previously, but had passed by because Otis felt his orange hair wouldn't fit with the group's sedate but polished visual image.

I hadn't seen Eddie Kendrick or David Ruffin for quite some time. I'd heard reports that Eddie was broke, or at least near broke, that Eddie's solo career was now in ruins, that he had lost his voice. So when Mary Wilson got a job working New Year's Eve 1984–85 at Detroit's Premier Theater and we discovered that Eddie Kendrick had been booked as the opening act, we were all—especially Mary—waiting to see what was going to come crawling through that door.

Well, when Eddie Kendrick walked very grandly into the theater that afternoon we were all shocked. It looked like the rumors of his condition had been false, because here was a perfectly preserved Eddie Kendrick, just like the dashing man we all remembered. When he went on stage that night in a simple but tailored suit, white shirt, and silk tie, and proceeded to do a twenty-minute or so show that was absolutely phenomenal, Mary and I stood in the wings along with the rest of her crew, mesmerized. With just a small, Detroit-based band behind him and no background singers, his voice stood alone—despite the fact that after the soundcheck, Mary's two unruly and unsupervised sons had had a field day playing with the controls on the sound board and had totally screwed everything up.

"Fuck it," said Mary. "Tony, someone will just have to fix it before tonight." But there was no time for a second sound check.

Eddie had already finished his performance and been well received, and Mary was in the middle of her regular Supremes show, when a beat-up Buick Electra 225 pulled up outside the backstage door. Out stepped a tall, skinny man in a suit, with a wide-brimmed hat cocked to the side, accompanied by a pretty young white woman. Next thing I knew a very subdued David Ruffin was standing with his arm around my shoulder, telling me how proud he was of Mary and me, and how pleased and surprised he was that Mary was able to do all this on her own after everybody had always said for years that she couldn't sing and had no real talent. "In the end she fooled them," he said. "Tony, in the end all us alley cats will fool them." He was very unassuming, very quiet—an altogether different David.

Later, when it was time for Eddie to join Mary on stage for a rendition of "Auld Lang Syne." I stood with David in the wings expecting him to jump up on the stage any minute and join in like he always used to do, invited or not. But he never made a move. Having been away from the stage for so long, he'd lost his confidence. He was a broken man—a man who'd blown a major opportunity, who'd spent four months languishing in jail, who'd been left with nothing, who hadn't learned how to live his life without getting into trouble except by hiding from trouble. Although he'd been living a dream of sorts—David had always loved horses and nature—he hadn't been living his life. His life was the stage and singing, and besides some songwriting and the occasional basement recording session in Detroit with Obie (Renaldo) Benson of the Four Tops, he'd had little to do with music.

I could see the sadness in David that night. It just wasn't like him to hang in the background. Even when Eddie announced from the stage that David Ruffin was in the house, and the screams rose up from the crowd, David was reluctant to go out on that stage. I had to just about push him out. But the moment he appeared in front of that crowd and heard them go wild, cheering him on to sing something, it was as if he lit up inside. Without a second thought, David started singing as if he had never stopped, and a whole jam session developed with him, Eddie, Mary, and her background singers all singing along to "My Girl" and "Ain't Too Proud to Beg" and all those old Temptations songs that David used to sing lead on.

It seemed so natural for them to be up there on the stage together. I too felt that same excitement all over again, those same butterflies in my stomach, and I could see that Eddie and David felt it as well. The whole thing came off like a huge extravaganza that had been rehearsed for weeks and weeks. It was a perfect ending to a perfect New Year's Eve. And before I knew it, Eddie Kendrick and David Ruffin had hooked up together and were out on the road as a duo. The legend would live on.

Chapter Four
Don't You Love Clowns?

The minute that Eddie Kendrick and David Ruffin got back together again as "former lead singers of the Temptations" their stars began to rise and their pockets began to fill. This reunion was hot news—too hot. Promoters, chastened by past experiences with David Ruffin, were scared to touch them. Deejays and fans, however, especially those from the *Big Chill* generation, quickly gave the two ex-Tempts the overwhelming support they needed, and before you knew it Kendrick and Ruffin were headlining, and Mary Wilson was very grateful to be opening for them.

I watched as the tables turned once again.

Of course, as each of these ex-Motown acts was almost guaranteed to attract its own, faithful crowd, promoters loved to throw a few of them together into one big package. They'd cheat and call it "Motown Revue," "A Reunion Tour," "Motown Legends on Tour." One of the most popular groupings of acts during those days featured Eddie Kendrick and David Ruffin, Mary Wilson of the Supremes, and Martha Reeves and the Vandellas—most memorably in the spring of '85, in Austin, Texas. It was a circus in three glorious, unpredictable rings!

The Texas tour kicked off without Martha Reeves. Starring the two former Tempts supported by "The Supremes featuring Mary Wilson," as she loved to be billed, the tour was chaotic from the beginning. From the very moment I heard the enormous ruckus descending the escalator at the airport in Texas and saw Eddie and David's band and entourage appear, I sensed trouble.

I'd been waiting for over an hour in the baggage claim area for them to arrive, trying meanwhile to placate a disgusted Mary Wilson, who kept insisting rather tragically that "a Supreme should never be kept waiting." Mary felt that her level of stardom had always exceeded Eddie's or David's; why should *she* of all people wait for *them*? But the promoter didn't care about varying heights of stardom or any of that. He had his profit margin to take care of, and wanted to economize by having us all crowd up on a big tour bus together, rather than let the individual groups go directly to the hotel as they arrived.

So we waited, and when we saw the former Temptations' band appear, hooting and hollering like they'd just been let out of a cage, Mary immediately warned me in no uncertain terms: "Tony, you just better make sure that none of my people fraternize with those animals. What trash and garbage! Look how they're carrying on!" Frankly, I thought they looked quite exciting.

Eddie and David came up behind the band. Well, when Mary got a look at Eddie her whole attitude changed, and she immediately went into her Norma Desmond in *Sunset Boulevard* mode with her back arched and her mouth barely opening to say a breathless "Hello, Eddie. How are you?" Eddie looked stunning in his ice-white, North-Pole-Alaska-glacier-white, not-a-mark-on-it jogging suit and white high-tops unlaced the way the young boys were wearing them, and a white leather baseball jacket with a matching cap turned back. Eddie was always impeccable. During the years I worked with him, I rarely saw him wear the same outfit twice. But forget about David. He looked like he was dressed for a dude ranch. This was Texas after all, but David resembled the cowhand not the rancher.

A shiny black, super-stretch limo arrived. The limo, it turned out, had been supplied for Eddie and David's use as stars of the tour. Next minute up crawled an old, rickety yellow school bus for everybody else, including Mary Wilson the Supreme. Luckily for Mary, Eddie and David were having none of that. They cursed out the promoter's representative and, like gentlemen, invited the Last Supreme to ride in the limo with them.

One double-false-eyelashed glance from Mary, and I reluctantly boarded the school bus with her band members. I could see the looks of disgust on their faces; they too were used to traveling in style, and when they saw how the former Temptations' band were acting, those looks only grew more disgusted because those guys were party guys, and with the horn section there were plenty of them. Personally, I thought they were a lot of fun. Eddie's close friend and able manager, Billy Bannister, was the life of the party. David had his own road manager too, Bruce, who claimed jokingly that he had once shot the great, wicked Wilson Pickett in the groin. As Mary's road manager, I wondered which one of us three would emerge as the main ringmaster.

The confusion progressed as the tour went on. We almost packed up and went home after the first show because the promoter didn't have enough money to pay us. But Mary thought the guy was cute, so she said that since this was his first time acting as a promoter, we should give him a chance to make up the money in the other cities on the tour. Eddie and David, who knew I wasn't shy about voicing my opinion, wanted to know what I thought. I told them,

"I'm for walking out. You guys know my unwritten rules: number one, no romance without finance; and number two, pay me before I start." Eddie roared with laughter.

The other two managers both agreed. "Sure. Tony's right. We're walkin' outta here."

"However," I said, "before you walk out—I don't know about *your* finances, but Mary really needs the money and wants to do the show."

"Fuck it," said David. "If Mary does it, we'll do it. We'll all stick together. And if that motherfucker doesn't pay, we'll all cut his balls off." Eddie, as usual, was more subtle, but nevertheless agreed with David. The old Motown family concept that Big Daddy Berry Gordy had so successfully instilled in their minds was still hard at work—that same mind-control tactic that he had used to keep everybody in line. Except now there was no Major Big Daddy around taking care of business and there was no line. There was just confusion developing at the fair.

So we did the next show, and the next, and by the time we got to Austin, where Martha Reeves was supposed to join us as the opening act, the confusion had reached a new peak. We found Martha plopped over the hotel check-in counter, trying to check in her group "with her wide backside stuffed in those filthy old sweat-pants," as Mary remarked—Mary, of course, was dressed in her best Supremes regalia.

Martha's huge wig was just slightly lopsided, and her sweatsuit ensemble looked like she'd slept in it. She probably had, since she and her band had driven all the way down from Detroit by van to save money. She had her brother with her as her road manager, who barely said a word during the whole tour, and two local back-ground singers who she would be using that night as Vandellas. They obviously thought they really were true Vandellas, because they were appropriately dolled up in a style that reminded me of the original Vandellas as they appeared on the cover of *Martha and the Vandellas Live,* circa 1967.

As soon as Mary had finished spying on poor Martha, she said, "Oh, please check me in Tony, and escort me, my dear, to my suite. I simply cannot be seen standing at a check-in desk like Martha." Eddie, David, and their crew, meanwhile, had come bouncing into the lobby and gone directly to take over the coffee shop.

In the midst of all the turmoil at the check-in desk, the "cute" promoter called up to say that ticket sales had been exceptionally slow; what should we do? I suggested to him that he call the radio stations and arrange for Eddie and David, Mary and Martha to take some call-ins and do on-air interviews as a way of promoting that evening's show. It was all arranged, and the limo arrived to carry the four "Motown Legends" to the radio station—at which Mary suddenly dug her worn spikes in and decided she wouldn't go: "I'm not going anyplace."

When I dared to ask why, she huffed, "I don't want to be bothered with that Martha Reeves, that's why. Furthermore," she said, gazing at her image in the mirror as she dusted loose powder onto her face, "Martha hates me because I look better than she does. Always did and always will!"

I went back and announced to the others, "Mary's not feeling very well. I think she's slightly dizzy. She's going to do a radio phone-in from her suite."

Instantly, Martha jumped in with, "Slightly dizzy? Oh, is that a fact, Tony? She's doing a phone-in from her little suite? Shit, well I'm not feeling good either. I just rode two days in a van from Detroit." And she hopped out of the limousine, leaving a silent David and Eddie behind.

"Tony," Eddie told me as he and David left for the radio station, "try to smooth things out between Mary and Martha so we can get through the night." They knew there was no point in arguing with Martha, because when Martha makes up her mind there's no changing it.

We were dealing with the same old petty jealousy, the jealousy that during the Motown years had revolved around the father figure, Berry Gordy, much to his total satisfaction it seemed. To whom was Berry paying more attention? Who was Gordy pushing for that number-one hit? Who was in favor today, this moment, this season? Martha Reeves had always felt that Gordy pushed the Supremes because of his intimate relationship with and apparent devotion to Diana Ross, despite the fact that Martha and her Vandellas were the girls with the real voices. It was as if, twenty years later, the spirit of the guru still haunted the lives and careers of these ex-Motowners—especially the women.

Later, at the theater-in-the-round where we were booked to do two shows that night, we decided that since quite a bit of our money would be coming straight from cash sales at the box office, we should send somebody to the box office to watch the cash flow. It looked like the best person for this job was David Ruffin's manager, Bruce, because of his continued boasting that he had once shot Wilson Pickett in the groin. We figured nobody was going to fuck with him. Anyway, Billy, Eddie's manager, had his hands full controlling the former Temptations' band as they roamed like uncaged animals all over the theater, and I was busy trying to keep Mary and Martha —or Demi-Diva Supreme and Grand-Diva Vandella as we loosely named them—out of each other's false cat claws.

The first show started. Martha, who had ended up doing the phone-in from the theater and had stayed on the radio for about two hours answering questions and generating interest, opened with her stand-in Vandellas, and worked the room for the twenty minutes for which she had been contracted. Next came Mary Wilson with her imitation "Supremes Show." She did about six it's-a-must costume changes and went over her scheduled time by about fifteen minutes.

Then Eddie and David came on and totally commanded the crowd. Offstage they were as different as night and day—Eddie, the boyish-looking one, quiet and intensely private; David, the bold one with a big heart. Onstage together they complemented each other perfectly. They were absolutely stunning.

Eddie and David opened the show together with a medley of about five Temptations hits, one after the other in rapid fire, with the two of them rotating leads and their band kicking plenty ass. As David was finishing the last song, Eddie shot up the ramp and did a lightning-quick costume change, ready to launch into his solo part of the show. Then David took over, singing all of his hits from the past. So you had three shows in one—the duo and the two solos—and the crowd went wild for it. It seemed to me at that point that if all went well, those two could build themselves into a major act again.

But for the time being, we still had our mounting money problems. David's manager came back from the box office and reported that the cash ticket sales for the night were far short of what we were all owed. What were we going to do? Everybody started popping up with different ideas. We should walk out. We should cancel the second show. We should do this. Let's fuck the promoter up. We should shoot him! (Don't you love clowns?)

David, with his blunt business sense, was getting extremely aggravated, motherfucking this and bitching about that and finally adding, "Let me tell you one fuckin' thing. I'm storming out."

I looked to Eddie to be his usual, level-headed self. I hadn't yet come face to face with that other side of him, the side that made what appeared to be snap decisions based on a mysterious logic only he understood, and a logic he never cared to explain.

"David, hold on a minute," said Eddie. "What we're going to do is, we're going to let the kid decide." After all those years, they still sometimes called me "the kid."

I felt both flattered by Eddie and shocked.

"Eddie, thanks," I said, "but I can't decide for everyone. You have Billy here and David has Bruce. I'm here as Mary's road manager. We're going to have to brainstorm and work it out together, and come up with a plan that will suit everybody." What was I saying?

"Tony, I've always had great confidence in you, so I'm leaving the whole situation in your hands," Eddie said. "What do you think, David?"

"He's about the only motherfucker here with any sense—I'm with it."

"How about you, Martha?" Martha didn't reply.

All eyes turned to Mary. Fluttering her hands like a charging bat trying to be a bewildered butterfly, she said in a semidramatic tone, "Well, I'll see." I looked around the dressing room and caught a glance of myself in the mirror.

As the new ringmaster, I knew that people were beginning to arrive for the second show. I was also positive that, as usual, we'd never see or hear from this promoter again since this was the last night of the tour. So I had to think fast, and I decided that the only equitable thing to do was to go on with the second show, take all the cash received that night, put it on the table, and cut it up equally four ways so that Eddie, David, Mary, and Martha could each go home with something.

David and Eddie were sitting up on the makeup table, taking it all in as I made my case. Mary was perched under the bare ceiling light bulb in a laughably striking pose. And then there was Martha, sitting on the couch with her brother, her lips sticking out a mile and her eyes locked on Mary. Almost everybody seemed to agree that this was the only way to go; this way, everybody could at least pay their band members.

All of a sudden, still staring directly at Mary, Martha said, "Well, I don't like it one fuckin' bit because after all, I came on this show with you people for one night, and Mary and Eddie and David have been working all week. You guys already made money."

She reminded us in no uncertain terms that we had flown into town, while she and her band had been forced to ride two days in a van. She said that as usual she wasn't being treated fairly, and launched into the familiar old story of how Berry Gordy and the rest of everybody at Motown had abused her over the years, trying to drive her repeatedly right over the edge. She said this was 1985, not 1965, and it wasn't Motown—she didn't have to be second to anyone. What was going to be done about her share of the money now? She wouldn't take less—not this time!

"Well, Martha," I said, "I think this is the fairest settlement we can reach at this time in view of the facts." I added that so far we had actually received very little cash from the promoter.

We waited. Suddenly and miraculously, with a certain look in her eye, Martha agreed to the settlement. She understood, and would be reasonable. It was done. Everybody had agreed, and I was just about to end the meeting when Mary Wilson decided out of the clear blue sky to take the floor and make a rambling speech, ending with "well, Tony, I really think that to be fair, since Martha came out here for a one-nighter and we did get some money for the other nights, we should give all of tonight's actual cash to Martha, since I'm sure Martha could really use the money." And she started carrying on with her "Let's feel sorry for Martha Reeves" movement. "Poor Martha. Girl, you know I always loved you. After all, Martha came all the way in an *old* van from home."

Eddie and David immediately agreed, which didn't surprise me. "Yeah, Mary, you're right," said Eddie. "That's the truth. That's the best thing. We're all from the same training school. We all worked our way up together, and you know, this is a family thing. Everybody is out here struggling."

"You know, Tony," David said, trying to smooth things over

because he could see that I had this I-made-a-big-mistake look on my face—"you know, what you said was the reasonable thing to do, the educated and fair decision. But some of this goes a little deeper than reason. This is more like a unity thing here. I like the way you run things strictly business, but Mary is right and I think we should go for what she said." It looked like the Supreme Court of one had handed down her decision.

So they went ahead and got the cash from the first show and handed it to Martha. Martha counted the money, recounted it, jumped up, put her hand on her hip, slipped the Dynel wig back on her head, and said, "I'm not doing no second show. I'm going home."

David Ruffin immediately jumped off the table and started calling Martha every crazy bitch, whore, and tramp in the book, while Mary stood there pretending to be shocked. Eddie just shook his head in calm disbelief and said, "Now, Martha, that's not fair. Why would you do a thing like that? Let's make a nice, happy evening of it—now calm down, David, hold on!" David had suddenly lurched forward and was trying to reach across and choke the shit out of Martha.

"Somebody snatch that money from that bitch," David was shouting. "She's crazy! Everyone knows Martha's crazy! She's been in the loony bin four or five fuckin' times. She's a fuckin' nut! Beat her ass! I said knock her out! I want my part of the motherfuckin' money back because she's a sick-in-the-head bitch!"

Eddie and Billy were trying to hold David back and stop him from jumping on Martha, who was now screaming, "You're not getting no goddamn money. And let me tell you something right now, Miss Mary Wilson, I went out and did my twenty minutes like my contract called for, and I got off. You went up there on that stage with your supposed-to-be Supremes shit, and nobody told you to do all those damn costume changes, parading up and down the ramp like a fuckin' model instead of a singer. You weren't even half-way singing. It was a total disgrace and you went over the forty-five minutes you were supposed to do by at least eight minutes."

"I'm outta here," she went on, "I done drove all the way from Detroit, tearing up my little bit of clothes out here, and you're not going to give me no attitude, Miss Thing."

Moving on to David and Eddie, she continued, "You two went up on the stage and you're supposed to be such big headliners, and all of a fuckin' sudden you don't know how to come off the stage—how come you get to sing every song the Temptations ever sung and go over your one hour set by twenty minutes? Plus, Eddie, your voice was weak and cracking!"

Eddie released his grip on David, at which David jumped at Martha and snatched the money from her, tearing some of it in the process. "Bitch," David said, "you're not getting paid till you go on the stage." But Martha just rustled up whatever money she could and left the dressing room in a hurry, followed by her forever silent brother.

By now the show was more than forty-five minutes late and the crowd was getting upset. The lights dimmed. Martha's band conductor started down the ramp to tell her musicians, who had been waiting in the pit to begin, that it was time to pack up and leave. But of course the audience took this as a sign that the show was finally going to begin and, with growing anticipation, started clapping and stomping. Martha's band in the pit suddenly got up. The audience now realized there might not be a show at all, and they got ugly fast.

"Okay," David said, "I'm going to get this whole thing cleared up right now."

Before any of us could say anything he dashed out the door and with a single, red spotlight on him he strode down the ramp, through the audience, and toward the rotating, dimly lit circular stage. The audience went wild.

"Ladies and gentlemen," he announced, "I would like to apologize because the show is extremely late. However, there have been some insurmountable financial problems that we had to get straightened out with the promoter. They have not been straightened out" (and at that people started booing the promoter). "They have not been straightened out to everyone's satisfaction. However, our managers, working together like a family as all of us Motown people do, have come up with a suitable arrangement that almost everybody has agreed with."

"But," he went on, "the financial arrangement was not to Miss Martha Reeves's satisfaction. And as you see, Martha has decided not to keep within the good nature of her fellow Motown recording artists and definitely not in the good graces of all you people who have waited so long. Martha Reeves has decided that she will not perform for our second show."

Boos filled the theater. People were striking matches in the darkness of the arena and chanting, "Down with Martha! Down with Martha!" David Ruffin just let it go. He let the audience build their chanting for a minute or so while he stood there, perfectly erect, center stage, right in the only spot of light in that whole, dark theater in the round, and when the boos reached their peak, just at the height of that moment he threw up his right hand to the sky, arched his left knee, and launched into "The Impossible Dream," from the Broadway show *Man of La Mancha.*

He did it in true, gravelly, David Ruffin style while giving all due respect to Paul Williams, who had sung lead on this song with Diana Ross in the "TCB" television special. He sang it *a cappella*; no music, no drums, no props, no nothing, and every note rang crystal clear. It was sheer Ruffin—a true showman, with a soft spotlight hitting his skeletal frame in a completely hushed theater.

As David hit the last note, holding the word "dream" for what seemed like an eternity while tears streamed down his face, the audience rose up like a massive butterfly leaving the cocoon. The fans were on the verge of mass hysteria. Security guards had to be rushed down to the stage to get David Ruffin through the adoring crowd.

It always amazed me how this man, who could hardly keep control of his own life, was able to confidently take control of an entire crowd of people. He had taken a bad situation—a big, hot, angry Texas mob—and he had turned it around. All the tension of waiting had been safely released. "Let the show begin!" yelled David as he vaulted up the ramp, and the audience went wild all over again.

With her band in place, Mary opened, very slowly and deliberately, singing the Beatles' hit "We Can Work It Out."

She descended the ramp, moving seductively toward an adoring audience in her gold lamé "Princess Grace" ball gown. At that moment Mary was in her full glory!

Later, back at the hotel, David banged on Martha's door. She, it turned out, had sat in the back of the audience throughout the second show. He called her a no-singing, hoarse-throated tramp, a tambourine-thumping project whore, and every other name he could dream up. Yet, although in the end Martha would leave Austin with cash in her pocket while everyone else left with postdated checks of questionable value, David and Eddie weren't really mad at Martha. No one was. Instead, they were hurt: "See how she treats us? See how she dogged us? What's the matter with Martha?"

The whole episode had become a big joke, too funny and too typical—"crazy Martha" had stayed too long at the fair and had gone and done it again. Before long, just about everyone was partying, laughing, drinking, and getting high. David and Eddie began their customary receiving of women bearing candies and flowers and pairs of panties, some oversized, with phone numbers written on them, while David's manager, Bruce, wandered around the hotel with a big smile, in his floor-length African dashiki, informing anyone who would listen that he was not wearing a fuckin' thing underneath it.

"Tony," he said, "weren't you there the time I shot that damn Wilson Pickett in the groin?"

"No, I was not," I laughed. "I don't remember ever being with you and Wilson Pickett."

"Yes you were. You were right there. I might shoot somebody tonight. What about Martha's brother?" he offered. "Let me get my motherfuckin' gun."

"No, no," I said. "That won't be necessary."

"By the way," said Bruce, "Mary wants you to get Eddie to come to her room." He smiled. I wondered.

I delivered the message to Eddie, who left the party immediately but returned from Mary's only ten minutes later.

Toward the end of the party there came a knock on the door.

"Who is it?" somebody asked.

"Dennis Edwards."

"Yeah, right, sure."

When I heard that name, I ran to the mirror to check how I looked, and then I ran to the door. "Let me see if this is Mr. Edwards," I said. "Because if it is, he must be greeted appropriately."

I opened the door. There stood a man who did indeed appear to be the one and only Dennis Edwards—but not the dashing, sophisticated Dennis Edwards who I remembered. His once sexy, muscular body had grown a little heavy with a nice stomach, and he looked like he had just come away from a hard day's work doing double shift in a factory. He had obviously met some hard times, which might or might not have been connected to some rumors I'd been hearing about Dennis and a lot of drugs.

"Hi, Tony," he said, as if I had just seen him yesterday, and he bounced right in. He hadn't been heard from in quite a while, and said he was just dropping by since he happened to be in Texas—to this day I have no idea what he was doing there. He seemed very relaxed, but not very happy, and mentioned more than once that he was looking to get back on the stage.

Dennis had been thrown out of Otis's group of Temptations once again for showing up late too many times and partying too much. When I heard the story, it seemed like the typical Motown-style firing. Dennis had shown up for work at some rehearsal space; looked through the window to see four Temptations working with another singer, Ollie Woodson; knew that Otis, Melvin, and others at the company were preparing Ollie to be his replacement; and walked away. In fact, as Otis tells it, Ollie had already been hired behind Dennis's back. But nobody had had the common decency to inform Dennis Edwards that he had just joined the growing ranks of ex-lead singers of the Temptations.

It was typical Motown. It was also typical Dennis. Who else would have just left and walked off into the sunset, without saying a word to anyone about the whole thing? As long as I'd known Dennis, all he had ever wanted was to make peace and to be liked by everybody. He hated confrontation or unpleasantness. No fuss, no fight. When I heard that story, I started to understand how a guy like Dennis could have stayed with Otis's group of Temptations all those years, just biting his tongue while Otis laid down the law.

Dennis didn't say anything about all of that as he joined the party. It was like old times again; nobody went to sleep that night. I would like to imagine that it was during these few hours that the idea was planted of David, Eddie, and Dennis getting together as a trio and forming a real three-ring circus of ex-lead singers of the Temptations. It certainly crossed my mind. It seemed the obvious way to go. Those guys had several things in common. They had all left the Temptations. They all knew big money, they all knew gut-bucket broke. They all knew that if they didn't make it now, that was going to be it for them. And they all knew that the odds were stacked against them making it alone.

Chapter Five
Motown Returns to the Apollo

he first time I ever saw the Temptations, the Supremes, the
Marvelettes, and a whole bunch of those early Motown Acts
performing was at the Apollo Theater in Harlem in 1962. I
was just ten years old at the time, and much more interested in
watching the really bad amateur acts than girls in little blue dresses,
or guys in tuxedos. I didn't even take in the names of those groups
that night. But it all came back to me a couple of years later, when
I met Florence Ballard and she told me about how she had come
to New York for the first time to perform at the Apollo, and how
nervous she had been to get on stage in front of all those people.
After that, the Apollo had a whole different meaning for me.

Twenty-two years later I was working as a road manager for Mary
Wilson, and doing well selling real estate. When I wasn't out on
the road with some tour, I divided my time between my house on
Long Island and an apartment on Manhattan's Upper East Side.
Once in a while I would pass the old Apollo Theater, now not much

more than a ghost on 125th Street, a rundown shell haunted by rich memories.

So, when word got out that the Apollo was to reopen after extensive renovations, I was very curious. And I wasn't the only one. This was big news, and it became clear immediately that the reopening would be one of the major show business events of 1985. A legend was being reborn. When you thought of the Apollo stage, you thought of all those great names like Ella Fitzgerald, Charlie Parker, Duke Ellington, Billie Holiday, Sarah Vaughan, Sammy Davis, Jr., Dinah Washington—and if you were a child of the sixties you thought of all the Motown stars who had gotten their start at the theater. So it came as no surprise to hear that the Apollo doors were going to be flung open again for the first time in years with a tribute to the Apollo's musical history as seen by Motown—"Motown Returns to the Apollo."

This was to be a special evening, a major production with hundred-dollar tickets and a list of invited guests that read like a who's who of New York and Harlem politics, the music world, downtown hip society, and of course, the black bourgeoisie. Anyone who had ever been anyone at the Apollo, and anyone who had ever been anyone at Motown, was going to be appearing in some form or another at this event—or so it seemed. I knew of at least three prominent people in Motown's musical history who had been overlooked—Eddie Kendrick, David Ruffin, and my then-employer, Mary Wilson.

The night before "Motown Returns to the Apollo" I was with Mary Wilson in New Orleans. Mary was appearing on a bill together with Anthony Gourdine of Little Anthony and the Imperials fame, and Martha Reeves and her Vandellas-for-the-night—Martha's two sisters, Lois and Delphine Reeves.

Once again, Martha was sizzling with those old Motown jealousies. Martha's emotions ran deep—being astrologically minded, I always believed it was because she was a moody Cancerian—but despite her occasional bouts of stubbornness I often found her to be quite compassionate. Tonight, though, she insisted on repeating to me her tired old stories about how Diana Ross had clawed and slept her way to the top and how Mary Wilson, who in her view had no real voice, had benefited as a Supreme from Diana's torrid affairs with Smokey Robinson and Berry Gordy. That, in Martha's view, was the sole reason that Miss Wilson was still able to perpetuate the Supreme's myth, even without a true vocal note in her well-worn throat.

It was an interesting web that Martha spun, a confusion of history and legend colored by her own brand of madness. And it seemed like the only satisfaction Martha could find in New Orleans was in the fact that she had been invited to perform the next night at "Motown Returns to the Apollo" while Mary had not. Like Eddie and David, Mary was on Berry Gordy's perpetual shit list—or so it was said. Besides, you couldn't have Otis's group of Temptations *and* David and Eddie, just as you couldn't risk putting Mary Wilson up on a stage with Diana Ross.

Well, Mary summoned the courage to go to the Apollo, invited or not. She bought herself a sensational, see-through black gown sprinkled with rhinestones and beading, and was all set to go and make a big splash at the opening. I was determined to go too; Martha told me to send for her if I had any trouble getting in: "I'll take care of you, Tony," she promised.

Late that night in New Orleans, when the performance was over and we were preparing to leave the next morning for New York City and the Apollo, I found the headstrong Lois Reeves in the hotel lobby looking like she was getting ready to punch someone out.

"That Martha! She pulled the same stunt again!"

I was wondering whether I was going to end up being a Vandella-for-the-night again, as I recently had been at the Westbury Music Fair on Long Island. A big fight had broken out between Martha and her nouvelle Vandellas, and they had refused to perform. When the promoter warned Martha, "No Vandellas, no pay," she had to come up with something quick.

I still remembered it vividly. The promoter had just left the room, and Martha had just finished cursing out her Vandellas as jealous bitches and whores, when she suddenly turned to me and said, "Tony, you don't sound that bad, and you know the Vandellas routine pretty well."

She looked at Danny, the president of the Martha Reeves Fan Club. "You certainly know all the moves me and the girls do," she told him. "You know what we're going to do?"

Martha had figured out a solution in minutes—quick thinking from a woman who many at Motown had long ago written off as crazy. That night, shortly after her opening number, Martha told the audience: "Everybody wants to be a Vandella, and tonight we're going to try something new." She began her next number, and with her cordless microphone she went around to members of the audience inviting them to sing background along with her. *Big Chill* crowds eat up shit like that. Then, just when she was getting ready to go into her medley of Martha and the Vandellas hits, she announced, "I would like to introduce my two newest Vandellas"—at which Danny and I shot down the ramp and onto the circular revolving stage to the sound of "Dancing in the Street." When the crowd saw that the "Vandellas" were guys they went completely crazy. We got a standing ovation, and Martha got paid!

Anyway, tonight was another night, and here was Lois Reeves again in a huff.

"Girl, what happened?" I asked her.

"Tony, you know Martha promised to fly me back to Detroit tomorrow morning so I could get home and have a day of rest before I go back to my job on Monday. I got work to do, honey, and I came out here making this little goddamn bit of money to help Martha out, because she couldn't have got this job if she didn't have her right Vandellas with her. Now she's done cussed everybody out—

you know how cheap Martha is—now she's saying I got to get in the van and ride all the way back to Detroit while she flies to New York."

"What van?" I asked her.

"Child, we didn't fly down here. Delphine and I rode down here in the fucking van with the band members. They picked me up at work on Friday, we drove all the way down here to New Orleans, we didn't get here until late Saturday afternoon, and we practically went right on stage. I was so freakin' tired, and my new costume was too tight, and if Martha thinks I'm leaving my good job and coming back on the road again to fuck around with her, she's wrong."

Martha was by now in her room behind closed doors, where she stayed until the next morning when it was time for her, Mary, and me to leave New Orleans for New York.

I wanted to get to the Apollo early because I knew that the security in Harlem would be intense that day. My brother Pierre, who had been hired as an Apollo dancer, had told me that to kick off the event the dancers would be boarding a special subway car on the A train line at 59th Street and Columbus Circle, would dance all the way to 125th Street to the accompaniment of Duke Ellington's "Take the A Train," then would dance down the block from the subway to the Apollo and straight up onto the Apollo stage. The whole thing was going to be taped for the upcoming television special, "Motown Returns to the Apollo."

I arrived to find Harlem looking like the Pope and the President of the United States were about to visit. There were police everywhere—in cars, on foot, on horseback, and with dogs. The Apollo's block was barricaded off to traffic; the only cars allowed through were the streams of limos that were arriving with stars and patrons, and the media vans that were coming to cover the event. You couldn't get anywhere near the stage entrance of the theater because 126th Street was also blocked off to anyone who was not part of the show.

Naturally, I had myself driven immediately to the rear entrance, where I told the guard that I worked for Mary Wilson. Naturally, he figured, A limo . . . Mary Wilson . . . the Supremes . . . Motown . . . open up the barricade. How was he to know that neither Mary nor I was supposed to be anywhere near there. Once Martha Reeves had graciously verified that I did indeed work for Mary Wilson, they issued me an all-access pass and in I sailed.

Inside, the theater was packed with stars and bigshots. Mary had already arrived and found a front-row seat, and the gossip had begun to roll like a vicious wave through the Apollo, along with the television cameras.

"Isn't that Mary Wilson sitting in the front row? I wonder if she's going to be part of the show."

"She's held up well!"

"After what happened at Motown 25! I'm surprised to see her here. Do you remember how Diana shoved her?"

"I wonder if she's had her face and tits done—she looks so good!"

"Fasten your seatbelts, it's gonna be a bumpy ride!"

The taping of the show went on for hours, with Bill Cosby as master of ceremonies introducing a whole string of huge production numbers. One of the more curious moments came when Boy George of the English group Culture Club stood up on stage with a seated Luther Vandross to perform as a duo. It was a glaring mismatch. Poor Boy George was so obviously petrified and out of place that Luther graciously carried the whole song almost by himself. After Gregory Hines had shown off in a long tap dance production number and Vanessa Williams, the recently dethroned nude Miss America, had done a fabulous tribute to Josephine Baker, Jennifer Holliday re-created her show-stopping song from *Dreamgirls* to an almost empty theater. She had arrived late—"I got very sick; I over ate," she announced as she arrived in the makeup tent. That song from

Dreamgirls came closer to the original Supremes than anything else Motown came up with that evening.

At last, during a break in the taping, Bill Cosby leaned down toward Mary. "How come you're not in the show?" he asked her. "How come you're not up here?"

"I wasn't invited," she told him.

"I'm going to put you up here in a place where they can't cut you out," he said.

He started announcing the stars for the next piece of the show, which was to feature Stevie Wonder singing his new song, "Part Time Lover." "Ladies and gentlemen," announced Bill Cosby, "Stevie Wonder. . . ." Everybody applauded like crazy. The Four Tops and two of Smokey Robinson's background singers stood up near Stevie, who was seated at the keyboard. And then, looking right at Mary, Cosby said, "Are there any more background singers out there?" And to everyone's surprise he helped her onto the stage. Mary got up there in her see-through gown and stood right next to the Four Tops' lead singer, Levi Stubbs, close enough so that there was no way the cameras could cut her out without cutting out Levi too. And of course nobody could say a thing about it.

I was standing near Motown president Suzanne De Passe at the time, watching the show on the monitors. When Mary got up on that stage Suzanne was outraged. "Your boss is out of her mind! That woman is crazy!" she screamed. "She turns up like a bad penny. What is she doing here?" She was doing everything in the world to get Mary edited out of the picture, but she must have known it was impossible. "Oh my God, why did he call her up? Gordy's going to have a fit!"

Berry was positioned regally on his front-row center seat in the mezzanine, but there was nothing he could do right then either— not even he was going to tell Bill Cosby to get Mary off the stage where Cosby had so conveniently put her.

I spent most of my time during the taping between the backstage area and the makeup tent that took up most of a small parking lot on 126th Street, watching the show on the monitors while I tried to catch everybody's comments. The major stars had their private RV trailers out in back of the theater, but the makeup tent was where the real action was. It was a bit like an old Motown picnic indoors, except everyone was older, and one hopes wiser. Some people were missing—those who had passed on, and those who had been passed by. Quite a few people were asking, "Where's David Ruffin? Where's Eddie Kendrick? This ain't the same without them. And for that matter, where's the Vandellas?"

Martha Reeves, who had had the foresight to bring in two huge bottles of white wine, was being surprisingly gracious to everyone —shockingly, even to Mary Wells. I remembered a minitour I had been on, during which Eddie Kendrick had assigned to me the thankless task of protecting Mary from Martha, who shared a dressing room. Martha had already drawn chalk lines across the dressing room floor to separate her area from Mary's; and she had taken a huge bunch of flowers delivered to Mary, ripped off the note, and claimed them as her own. To top it off, Martha had thrown Mary's gown on the floor.

It was the last thing Mary Wells needed. She was there with her baby girl, Sugar, and an abusive husband, trying to hide the fact that she was sick and aging and seriously strung out on drugs, and all she said about Martha's crazy behavior was, "Why is she doing this to me? Why does she hate me? I like Martha." My heart always went out to Mary, who, despite the fact that her glory days were long over, marched on against all odds.

It seemed odd that for all the production and hoopla surrounding "Motown Returns to the Apollo," neither Martha Reeves nor Mary Wells had been given much more than sixty seconds or so on stage. The non-Motown people were the ones who had the big production numbers, and some of the patrons later complained that they would have preferred to have seen a full medley by the Temptations, including Ruffin and Kendrick, rather than a Rod Stewart tribute to Otis Redding.

Boy George, who always appeared in his unique form of drag, was hanging out backstage, dressed in a big plaid coat-dress type of thing and huge, unpolished combat boots, looking nervous and entirely out of place. His sidekick-in-drag, Marilyn, a less successful English male singer, seemed totally star-struck by all the Motowners. Later in the evening, Luther Vandross came up to me and asked to be presented to Mary Wilson. He told me he was nervous, and seemed thrilled that he was about to meet one of the original Supremes, which I thought was a refreshing attitude coming from a superstar. Sarah Vaughan was there too, acting "like a prima donna and looking like a baboon in a cheap wig," as someone said. Jennifer Holliday came into the tent dressed in miles of fabric, and was immediately surrounded by well-wishers, which didn't stop her from grabbing a whole tray of hors d'oeuvres from a passing waiter and proceeding to eat the whole thing, balancing the tray on one hand while she talked.

I was still in the makeup tent when I heard Bill Cosby announce over the monitors, "Ladies and gentlemen, we have a special guest—" at which someone in the tent shouted, "Oh God, I knew it. The bitch has arrived."

"It must be the Boss, Diana Ross," someone added.

Diana had just flown in by helicopter from Atlantic City, where she had been performing at one of the top casinos. By now it was so late, and the day had been so long, that people had already begun to leave their seats. Diana was just in time to make her grand entrance for the closing number of the show.

With what she tried to pass off as casual breathlessness she took the stage and started to sing the Foreigner song, "I Want to Know What Love Is." Her voice sounded raspy, thin, very high, and off-key. She had to do several takes because she apparently did not know all the lyrics to the song. Perhaps she felt as embarrassed as the audience did for her, because after a few false starts, as the stars began to file on stage to join Diana in this closing number, she handed the mike to Patti LaBelle as if to ask for help. Patti just smiled and took over the song, vocally murdering an unhappy Diana Ross.

The taping was followed by a formal dinner of soul food in a huge, tented school yard behind the Apollo. The white dinner tent must have been about half the size of a football field, all done up with red carpet and white linen and lavishly decorated, Shah of Iran–style.

"Look, there's Berry and Diana," I warned Mary Wilson as I caught sight of the duo across the room.

We started to approach them very slowly and deliberately. They were about forty feet away from us and floating through the crowd, apparently unaware that they were headed in our direction. The press anticipated the reunion that was about to happen, and started to cluster like bees to honey. We kept strolling as the crowd grew. Seconds later Berry saw us.

"You've been spotted, girl," I whispered to Mary.

Mr. Gordy kept moving toward us with Diana, slightly behind him, looking worriedly over his shoulder. What must have taken but a minute seemed to last an eternity. Finally Mary Wilson and Berry Gordy were face to face. The wayward child had met her maker. They both stopped—in fact, the whole tent seemed to be momentarily suspended in time. A second later the press was clamoring around them, freezing the moment.

"Mary, you look wonderful tonight," said Gordy, extending his arms with a smile. That was all. He gave no indication of being even slightly annoyed that Mary had had the nerve to show up.

Mary, however, didn't return his politeness. "Well, Berry," she hissed, "how did you expect me to look? Old, like you?"

If it hadn't been for the sound of cameras flashing you could have heard a pin drop. Even I, who had come to expect anything from Mary, was taken aback by her gracelessness. She had broken an important rule, often quoted at Motown: Good manners can take you places money cannot.

Diana was still standing behind Gordy for protection, looking like she was scared that Mary was going to fight her, "Detroit Style."

"Hi, Diane," Mary said breezily. "How are ya'?"

"Hi," said a wide-eyed Diana from over Gordy's shoulder as she flicked her fingers through her wild mane of hair. And then, tugging at his arm, she quickly said, "Let's go, Berry," and they were out of there, leaving a smiling but mute Mary encircled by a pack of stunned photographers.

It had been a fabulous evening, a fabulous production. All those stars in one damn place at one time—it was like heaven to me. Disgusted as I was at the way Motown had treated Eddie, David, and Mary, I knew that, once again, it was really thanks to the incredible Motown machine that an event that could have been pure chaos had turned out to be such a success.

Chapter Six

Too Radical, Too Black

"Motown Returns to the Apollo" may have been the gala that reopened the theater, but it had been closed to the general public. For the premiere of the theater as an ongoing venue, a surprising choice had been made. Two weeks after the Motown taping, Daryl Hall and John Oates, a top white pop duo, would perform to benefit the NAACP. Hall and Oates are considered pioneers of "blue-eyed soul"—white guys singing black music. They had been on the scene for years and were riding on a string of big hits that attracted a sizable black following. Yet the idea of two lily-white boys opening the Apollo, of all places, to the general public—boys who moreover had appeared on album covers in full makeup—immediately provoked controversy. It was big news, and the show was sold out almost as soon as it was announced.

I had not intended to see Hall and Oates. And I probably would never have noticed Eddie Kendrick and David Ruffin's names splashed across the Apollo marquee right under "Hall and Oates" if I hadn't decided that day to have my driver drop my brother Pierre off for rehearsals at his job as an Apollo dancer.

I could hardly believe it. The last time I saw Eddie and David they were kind of beat. We were on that minitour in Texas. They were arguing with the promoter and counting the night's takings because the promoter wasn't going to pay. Now they were riding high. What had happened?

I jumped out of the limo without even waiting for the driver to stop and ran into the building, busting right through the doors to the theater. I could hear the Temptations' music coming from inside. There were Eddie and David, sitting in the front row, watching the band rehearse. They looked as if they had just stopped in at an exclusive mens' shop on their way from the health spa. I hadn't seen Eddie or David in a few years. We hugged and kissed and I sat right down, ready for the latest gossip.

David and Eddie were back. Now, instead of traveling in tour buses and staying in flea bag hotels, they were riding in a vintage automobile straight out of a gangster movie. They were staying in extravagant hotel suites overlooking Central Park. They looked like a million dollars, Very Motown. They looked like they used to look, way back in the days when Motown really was the Sound of Young America, when practically every record went gold, when it seemed like the good times would never come to an end.

Between sound checks and decisions and viewing selections of outfits that were being sent over by the very expensive clothier next door, Eddie and David began to fill me in on what had happened. The story started back in the sixties, at the Uptown Theater in Philadelphia. Daryl Hall and John Oates were playing in a band that opened for the original Temptations. Both Hall and Oates had always loved the Tempts—in fact, they'd always claimed to have been brought together by this shared musical passion. Daryl Hall in particular had been fascinated by their music and started to hang around them.

In time, Hall grew very close to Paul Williams, who would once in a while give him his old stage outfits to wear. One time, David, the Capricorn Prince, did one of his no-shows and Hall stood in for him, becoming a Temptation-for-the-night as I had once become a Vandella-for-a-night.

Twenty years later their heroes from the original Temptations were split up, scattered, and struggling. Although Hall and Oates were big stars, Hall had become something of a recluse, often hiding away on his estate in New York State. He needed a boost, something to get him excited about performing again. They decided to spice things up by reuniting the living original Tempts—Melvin Franklin, Otis Williams, David and Eddie—and bring them out on the road.

As the story goes, Hall and Oates first approached Otis, who declined the offer. After the 1982 Temptations reunion tour, he had had enough of Eddie and David. But Hall and Oates were not interested in working with just Otis and Melvin. They were in particular fans of David Ruffin, not only as a performer but also for his bad boy reputation. So Hall and Oates offered Eddie and David the deal that they had originally planned to offer all four Tempts.

Eddie didn't hesitate. This was a big opportunity—a show at the Apollo, followed by a national tour playing to sellout crowds in major concert arenas, with tons of media exposure. Someone was knocking on their door, ready and willing to pull them through. What's more, Hall and Oates's record company, RCA, would be releasing a *Live at the Apollo* album, which meant additional exposure for Eddie and David.

But David wasn't sure. He'd been living on a friend's horse farm in Michigan for three years. There had only been the occasional, small-time engagement in the short time since he'd been back with Eddie. He didn't have the right clothes for a big tour—he didn't even have a tuxedo—and he didn't feel that he was in shape. Perhaps he was also reluctant because he wasn't sure he was ready to jump back into the old lifestyle. He had been far away from limos and groupies and all the trappings of stardom, far away from drugs and alcohol. He knew how destructive success could be for him. But then again, David needed to perform. That's what made him feel like a whole person.

David called his brother, Jimmy Ruffin, and told him about the wardrobe problem. Jimmy told him to call Hall and Oates and explain, and they would take care of the tux, the money, all of that—which they did. The contracts were signed, and a series of meetings were held to discuss the tour. Naturally, David didn't show up on time for any of those meetings.

Despite all of that, the Apollo show was a huge success. The album recorded that night ultimately went gold. Hall and Oates acted like the perfect hosts—although in fact the Apollo stage was more of a home to Eddie and David than it was to the white duo. Eddie was introduced as "a special and dear friend," and David as "the voice you love." For their cameo appearance, Eddie and David did two leads each, singing their original Temptations hits with Hall and Oates singing the background parts and loving every minute of it. The audience went wild.

Everybody was thrilled. After the show we all went into what had been the makeup tent for "Motown Returns to the Apollo" and was now the dinner tent, where the patrons with high-priced tickets could meet and greet the stars. Eddie and David were very optimistic, very up. I couldn't believe that this was happening. It was as if they had won the lottery. As they climbed into their vintage limo and I watched them get driven away, I thought, "I hope somebody doesn't fuck this up by 'tying one on'."

During the following months I was kept very busy working for Mary Wilson. She was doing okay, though not as well as she would after her book, *Dreamgirl*, reached the best-seller lists in 1986. That's when she started getting better-paying, higher-class gigs, including one opening for Bill Cosby in Atlantic City.

I'll never forget that night. Mary and I were in her dressing room when a security guard knocked on the door and announced that a Mr. Davis would like to see her. I said, "Who the fuck is that?" Mary didn't have a clue who this Mr. Davis was either, so I poked my head out the door and waited until I saw a tiny, decrepit man with a cane hobbling down the hallway from Cosby's dressing room.

I quickly shut the door and waited for him to knock. When I opened it for him I had to look down on the man—that's how short he was. In that instant, when this old guy looked up at me, I realized who he was. I slammed the door in his face and screamed to Mary, "Oh my God, it's Sammy Davis, Jr.!"

Mary came running out of the bathroom screaming, dressed only in a pair of black fishnet nylons and a long black tafetta evening skirt, and ducked back again while I opened the door and called to her, "Mary, Mr. Davis is here to see you."

She waltzed back into the room, still completely topless. I just about died, but Sammy smiled and said, "What a great way to greet someone!" As Mr. Davis proceeded to offer Mary a few lines of cocaine, I just stood in shock at the sight of her snorting coke bare-breasted in front of an aging Sammy.

"What's the matter with you, Tony?" Mary hissed at me before asking me to leave the room. "These ain't the kind of thing that my man Sammy hasn't seen before."

Although in 1985 Mary wasn't as successful as Eddie and David were rapidly becoming, she was working hard and keeping me busy. I could only wonder how things were going for Eddie and David, and whether David was about to go off into one of his drug binges as he tasted success. He had told me, "I'm gonna stay straight this time, Tony. I'm staying away from those drugs. I'm gonna take the cure."

From what Eddie had told me, their schedule was packed with appearances, including Live Aid in Philadelphia which was definitely the highlight of the tour. With the companion concert in

London, the televised show was the biggest live music broadcast ever, and a very successful charity event. Hall and Oates went on at prime time, and the pledges during their segment were the highest for the whole show. Years later, when the Tempts were inducted into the Rock and Roll Hall of Fame, Eddie would remember that night in Philadelphia as just about the only other time he had ever felt as good.

Wherever they went, Eddie and David were given superstar treatment—Hall and Oates supplied them with just about everything they could possibly need. Years after their Motown heyday, Eddie and David were once again being treated as if they were somebody's treasure. "The suites are so big you can't hardly hear when someone's knocking on the door," David told me. When they weren't on stage, they were still working hard doing radio and television talk shows. As time went by, however, it seemed as if David and Eddie didn't really want to work that hard. Eddie's voice wasn't holding up well. David's weakness for drugs recurred to no one's surprise, least of all David's. His asthma was so bad that he had to be hospitalized for respiratory failure. Neither he nor Eddie wanted to have to fly some place on their off days to do ten minutes of early morning radio or television interviews. But they went grudgingly.

Despite all of this, Hall and Oates's label, RCA, offered Eddie and David a recording contract to do their own album. Eddie told me that some songs were recorded over and over again before the album was finally mastered. David didn't like anything they were doing. He didn't like the songs, he didn't like the arrangements, he didn't like the background singing, he didn't like a thing. "Tony," he told me, "RCA is giving us no control over any goddamn thing on this album."

When David showed up at RCA with songs under his arm that he had written, produced, and recorded, the company refused to put them on the album. They said they were too radical. "Too black,"

David said. Both he and Eddie complained bitterly that the company was looking for too much of a white, pop sound. RCA, who had been very patient, now counter-complained that Eddie and David should wake up and be happy with what they were getting.

Everybody bitched about everybody else. It was an atmosphere that provoked people to wonder who needed whom. David, who now had plenty of money to blow on cocaine and a lifestyle to accommodate his highs, started missing recording sessions, so Eddie had to lay down tracks by himself. When David did show up he raised hell over money that he claimed was owed him. It was a pattern that soon became David's own kind of vicious circle. Promoters and producers would hold back money so that David would show up, and David wouldn't show up because he was not getting paid. It was all down to who controlled whom.

Then John Oates decided to get all wrapped up in things, adding lyrics and background vocals to a song that Eddie had cowritten, which in Eddie's opinion totally fucked it up. Somehow, Eddie decided that he and David were being exploited. Hall and Oates, he said, were ripping them off and prostituting them in order to achieve acceptance from the black audiences.

I started to wonder if Eddie's experiences with Motown had left him overly sensitive to feelings of being used and abused, especially during the following years when I would often notice him getting very bitter if the Hall and Oates episode was mentioned.

Once, when I was spending a night out on the road, I asked Eddie again what had happened with Hall and Oates to get him so upset. His answer made no sense whatsoever. Each sentence was an incomplete thought, no sentence followed on from the last, and in the end I decided better to let it go. I knew I would never find out what had really happened, and as far as I could see these two former Tempts were making more money than they had seen in years, thanks to Hall and Oates. But the bitterness was there. In

Eddie's mind, both RCA and Hall and Oates were only interested in using them.

David's feelings about the Hall and Oates episode were different, though equally negative. "I don't mind being used," he said, "but pay me!" More than that, David was concerned about the spiritual aspects of the experience. He told me later that Daryl Hall was interested in the occult.

"No doubt about it," David said, "Jesus Christ is the answer to all our questions. And remember, you can only reach the Father God through His son, Jesus Christ."

RCA, meanwhile, was losing its patience. It was finally sinking in that they had one ex-Tempt who worked his butt off but could hardly sing any more with that little squeaky voice of his, and another ex-Tempt with a sensational voice but who was completely unreliable.

There were ego problems too. A single that Eddie had helped write, "One More for the Lonely Hearts Club," was released and started climbing up the charts. When RCA wanted to release as a second single one of David's solo songs, Eddie threw a shit fit and said he would quit.

By the time the album came out, the record company had written off David and Eddie, and did nothing to promote it. They weren't interested in coaxing and pampering two washed up ex-Tempts the way Berry Gordy had done years ago. Gordy had massaged their egos so that they would go into the studio and do exactly what he or their producers wanted them to do.

By the end of it all, everybody felt like they had been raped and used big time. Just as Eddie and David felt used by Hall and Oates, Hall and Oates probably felt used by Eddie and David.

Almost as soon as they had finished the tour, Hall and Oates apparently wiped their hands of Eddie Kendrick and David Ruffin, who instantly dropped out of their luxury bubble and fell back into reality. After playing a sold-out tour and releasing a live album that went gold—all in a matter of months—they were suddenly out in the very same cold from which they had been rescued.

Some years later Eddie and David were once again paired with Hall and Oates on the occasion of the Temptations' induction into the Rock and Roll Hall of Fame. The ceremony was held at New York's Waldorf-Astoria Hotel on January 18, 1989—David's forty-eighth birthday. It seemed as if all was forgiven if not forgotten between the two duos. At least they made a good effort to hide their grievances from the cameras and crowds. Hall and Oates graciously presented the Tempts with the honor, joining them in singing the classic hits once again. David told me that offstage he joined Mick Jagger and Keith Richards in a community crack pipe that the three circulated amongst themselves.

The real tensions now were between the two groups of Tempts who were sharing the honor of induction. First of all, none of our group could figure out why Dennis's replacement in the group, Ollie Woodson, as well as Paul's replacement, Richard Street, and Eddie's replacement, Ron Tyson, had been brought along. In fact, the whole thing got so confusing with all these former and current Temptations strutting about that the media couldn't figure out who was getting inducted and who wasn't. There was talk that Melvin and Otis had been banking on a no-show by David and Eddie, and had brought their trio of replacements along just in case. Otis Williams had recently published a memoir, *Temptations*, that was rough on Eddie and David. Otis insisted on a separate table for himself and Melvin Franklin, who was there against doctor's orders. He had been a sick man lately. It was four or five years since I'd first heard him talk about how rough it was to go on stage sometimes, because of various aches and pains. He had chronic rheumatoid arthritis—so bad that at times he could hardly stretch his fingers out. But the Temptations were doing too well for him to quit. Unlike our former Temptations, who were lucky to get four jobs a month, they were working consistently and it was good work. Those guys were making money. Besides, Otis without Melvin was inconceivable.

Dennis Edwards was in the middle, as usual. He was back with Otis's Tempts, but the very next day he would appear on a local TV talk show with David and Eddie. Since Otis still insisted on putting himself forward as exclusive spokesman for his group of Temptations, this was a rare opportunity for the naturally talkative Dennis to get a word in.

Later, when Cindy Birdsong of Diana Ross and the Supremes fame discovered that Dennis Edwards had been inducted into the Hall of Fame, even though he had not been an original member of the Temptations, she immediately called the organizers to find out why she, as Flo Ballard's replacement in the original Supremes, had not been inducted the previous year along with a very present Mary Wilson and a very absent Diana Ross. She was stunned to discover that Mary Wilson had insisted on her exclusion from the Supremes' induction; if they allowed Cindy in, Mary would refuse the honor.

"Damn!" a friend of mine put it when he heard the story. "Despite all that etiquette training and talk of family loyalty, some of those Motown stars can really be vipers."

Chapter Seven

Dennis, Open This Motherfuckin' Door!

It was a glorious Mother's Day weekend in 1989. I was up from my new home in Florida, sequestered at the penthouse in New York and busy working on my first book, *All That Glittered: My Life with the Supremes*. Now that I had quit working for Mary Wilson, my links with Motown were almost broken. I had left Mary in December 1987, after a long European tour during which she had grown so bitchy and abusive that I knew I either had to quit right there or end up in jail for plunging a knife through her heart. So, after two years off the road, I felt as if I had almost left Motown far behind me. But I was learning that legends don't fade easy. I'd been thinking about that Evermore-a-superstar attitude that nearly all the Motown artists I had ever known seemed to maintain, even in their least starry times, which in turn reminded me of a story involving the not-so-Supreme Mary.

The story takes place in the early eighties. Mary is giving an impromptu party in the small, hot New York apartment of one of

Mary's most devoted fans and disciples. Around two in the morning, she asks me, "Tony, I'm completely out of C-sharp. Can you just run right out and get me some?" As if I know every small-time drug dealer in the city—a true jack-of-all-trades.

Mary was very fond of her cocaine, or C-sharp as she fondly called it. She had very little money to spend on drugs in those days, but her friends and devotees were only too happy to pay for her supply because they knew from experience that the higher Mary got, the happier she was to dog Diana Ross. It could be a lot of fun.

Being somewhat unfamiliar with how to score drugs, I call a friend of mine who travels in those dark circles, and together we drive to a certain street in the city where you can buy whatever you want from the safety of your car. Nevertheless, I feel like I'm risking my life as I hand over the money and am given a small packet in return, and I'm more than upset when, on my return, Mary starts screaming at me that she's been ripped off.

We argue for a half an hour while she snorts every bit of the stuff I brought her, and then she demands that I go back to the same street corner and get some more—at a discount. "And this time, Mother Mary is going to go with you," she tells me.

With Mary all bunched up in the back seat of the Mercedes, sucking on a bottle of cheap champagne, we return to the scene of the crime. The same dude who sold me the cocaine comes over to the car. Next thing I know, Mary's sticking her head out of the car window and asking the guy, "Hey! Do you know who I am?" like she's doing an American Express commercial.

"Lady, what the fuck do you want?" The guy's looking at her like she's crazy.

"I'm one of the Supremes!" Mary tells him. I'm telling myself, We're dead.

For some reason the guy seems interested in Mary's antics.

"My momma used to listen to the Supremes when I was a kid,"

he tells her, "so if what you're saying is true then I'm willing to let you prove it." At which point Mary launches into a full rendition of "Stop! in the Name of Love." She sings lead, with all the hand movements and everything. Meanwhile, the traffic is backing up behind us, the dealer has invited a bunch of his friends to come over and share the experience, and I'm in a complete panic.

Mary, however, seems completely relaxed. She finishes the song and tells the man, "That $100 piece these guys bought from you earlier—it's not big enough. I've been all around the world, and that was the smallest $100 piece I ever saw in my life. I want a discount."

The crowd around the car is skeptical and getting nasty. "She ain't no fuckin' Supreme," says one guy. "That bitch is scammin' on us."

"What are you? One of the background babes?" says another.

"Are you in drag? She's probably a narc."

"Sing something, bitch!" two more guys mock in unison.

Time to make a move, I'm thinking. But by now a jeep has pulled around the corner and blocked our exit.

Mary starts sings "Reflections" in the back of the Mercedes, and once again demands a discount. To my surprise, they eventually settle on $75, and we split.

"Honey," Mary tells me in a haughty tone as we head back to her crony's apartment, "You got to let them know who you are. Allowances are always made for stars. Asshole, don't you know that by now?"

I had to laugh, remembering this story, and yet it was as sad as it was funny. It was almost as if Berry Gordy and his Motown system had hypnotized these people into a kind of charmed dream world in which they were demigods, immune to any of life's harsher realities. And they had never woken up.

My thoughts were interrupted when the phone rang. It was my sister, Ramona.

"Tony, you want to go to a concert tonight at the Beacon Theater?"

"Who's going to be there?"

"The Temptations."

"Really? Which Temptations?" By now I had learned that the billing "The Temptations" could mean any likely or unlikely combination of men.

"Well, it says in the paper, David Ruffin, Eddie Kendrick, and Dennis Edwards, former lead singers of the Temptations."

"What! Those three are together? Good God! Listen: it's about one o'clock now. I'm gonna call a limo to take me over to their sound check. I'll get back to you later, girl!" Evidently, yet another link was about to be formed in the Temptations chain.

News of both Eddie and David had been pretty thin since their falling out with Hall and Oates. All had seemed strangely lost after that highly successful tour. Unfortunately, about the only recent news was of David being thrown brutally into a Detroit jail one spring night in 1988 after the police found cocaine on him. But David had been arrested so many times for one reason or another that this was no longer big news; it was rather routine.

As I later learned, right after the Hall and Oates experience in 1985, David had returned to the safety of the horse farm to try and pull his life back together. He knew he had blown it big-time. He knew he had blown it for Eddie too. He had let him down, and at that moment Eddie didn't want a thing to do with him or his problems. That was the way their relationship went, it was a pattern. I never knew for sure whether Eddie was really as hard-hearted as he sometimes seemed, hardly calling David or showing any interest until David was straight again and Eddie needed him, or whether it was just the strong survival instinct of a man who thought that he could lead his life separately from everyone else's.

Eddie had always been pretty moralistic; he thought he could get closer to God by cutting himself off from contaminating influences. Eddie would say things like, "You have to avoid being around evil, because evil just drags you down and stops you finding inner peace"—and to Eddie, evil meant anything that caused problems in the world, including drugs and people who did drugs. I'd also heard him say that you can never really know another person, just the side they choose to show you.

David was spiritual too, but in a completely different way. He didn't judge people by the way they lived their lives—how could he? He had marked in his Bible that famous passage from Paul's letter to the Corinthians: "So faith, hope, love abide, these three; but the greatest of these is love." So when David showed the side of himself that Eddie couldn't deal with, that's who Eddie thought David was. He never seemed to understand the addiction.

When, after the Hall and Oates debacle, David fled back to the safety of the horse farm, his girlfriend Debbie and a longtime friend named Margarette implored him to seek treatment for his addiction. They were worried about David's health. David always said, "I'm not gonna die. I know what I'm doing." He thought he was going to live to ninety or a hundred like his uncle. But finally he agreed to allow a drug counselor to come to the farm and talk to him. With the counselor came someone from Eddie and David's booking agency, who told David that if he didn't get treatment she would stop getting him work. After talking to the counselor for about six hours David agreed to go into treatment at a private center in New York.

David stayed at the clinic for several months, becoming more enthusiastic by the day. This was a total treatment plan—he got a complete physical workover, drug education, detox, and psychotherapy. During therapy sessions he delved into himself, his past, his weaknesses, his regrets. He discovered that he wasn't really crazy. Lots of times he had thought he was off the rails, because why else would he keep doing something he knew was killing him?

David had started to understand addiction as a disease. He even talked about opening his own drug treatment center up at the farm so he could help other addicts. That way, he told Debbie, she'd have lots of people to help with the horses. David wanted everyone, especially Eddie, to visit him at the center and see for themselves what a wonderful thing it was. He wanted Eddie to see where he went back to every night, and why he felt safe there. Maybe he thought that if Eddie came, Eddie would learn how to help him.

When there were bookings, David traveled with a counselor from the center who waited backstage for him and made sure no drugs reached him. It was a whole new way of life. He kept pretty much to himself and started to take care of putting his life back together. He discovered that he didn't need the drugs in order to perform. In fact, he began to see how drugs affected his ability to perform, and through that his self-respect.

Sometime during the winter David went back to the farm for a Christmas break and never returned to treatment, although his counselors felt he had plenty more work to do. He said he didn't need treatment anymore, he was fine, he had it all under control, and he couldn't afford it. Maybe he'd been listening to Eddie and some of the guys in the band who'd been telling him, Man, you don't need that shit. I don't see why you're spending all those thousands and thousands on that.

"All you need is willpower," Eddie would tell him. In private, Eddie was known to say, "David will never get off drugs. He's the devil incarnate."

Eddie was living part of the time with his mother down in Birmingham, Alabama, in the home he had bought for her. The rest of the time he stayed with a woman in Atlanta, where he spent his days hanging out at the local barbershop, shooting the breeze with the regulars. Being Eddie, he never spoke to anyone in his professional life about his Atlanta life. I didn't even know he had a child down there until the kid was about three years old. I never could really understand why Eddie kept the pieces of his life so separate.

I heard that even his own mother complained that she hadn't seen her grandchild more than two or three times.

Neither Eddie nor David had been working much; they must have been living off the money they'd made with Hall and Oates. As for Dennis, the last time I had seen him was in Austin, Texas, when he had shown up out of the blue in Eddie's hotel room looking well-worn and decidedly out of shape—truly not routine for Mr. Dennis Edwards, a man I fondly call "The Last Star"!

In the years since that encounter in Texas, Dennis had recorded an unsuccessful solo album for Motown and toured his solo act in some small clubs. Eventually, he had been invited back in through the revolving door of Otis Williams's Temptations after his replacement, Ollie Woodson, was fired for bad-mouthing the Tempts behind their backs and showing up late or not at all too many times. Then Dennis was fired again for—no surprise—not showing up, and Ollie was rehired. It was getting to seem like déjà vu in that group.

I started thinking about all the different lineups they'd had over the years, and I decided to make a list because I thought maybe they could have broken some world record of hirings and firings in a singing group—as far as I knew, Eddie was the only Tempt who had left eagerly. The others were all thrown out for bad behavior of one sort or another, except Eddie's original replacement, Richard Owens. He simply couldn't cut the mustard and was let go only a couple of months into Otis's eighteen-month probation period for new "personnel."

Anyway, this is what the list looked like:

1961   Eldridge Bryant, Eddie Kendrick, Paul Williams,
        Otis Williams, Melvin Franklin.
1964   David Ruffin, Eddie, Paul, Otis, Melvin.
1968   Dennis Edwards, Eddie, Paul, Otis, Melvin.
1971   Dennis, Richard Owens, Richard Street, Otis, Melvin.
1971   Dennis, Damon Harris, Richard, Otis, Melvin.

1975	Dennis, Glenn Leonard, Richard, Otis, Melvin.
1976	Louis Price, Glenn, Richard, Otis, Melvin.
1979	Dennis, Glenn, Richard, Otis, Melvin.
1982	David, Eddie, Dennis, Glenn, Richard, Otis, Melvin.
1983	Dennis, Glenn, Richard, Otis, Melvin.
1983	Ollie Woodson, Ron Tyson, Richard, Otis, Melvin.
1986	Dennis, Ron, Richard, Otis, Melvin.
1989	Ollie, Ron, Richard, Otis, Melvin.

That made fourteen different lineups, and fourteen different men all of whom could claim to be current or ex-Temptations, with Ollie and Dennis replacing each other every few years, and Otis and Melvin always bringing up the rear. Where the other replacements came from or went to, I don't know—maybe they had a temp agency for Tempts. I never heard of any of them after they stopped being Temptations.

I had no idea what Otis's latest group of replacements had been up to—I really had no interest in them. They'd become a glittery Vegas-style act that appealed to an older crowd. They still did the classic Tempts hits, but their dance steps had been toned down to a bare minimum by now because neither Otis nor Melvin were in too good shape, and the replacement voices just didn't have the excitement of the original Temptations. I'd seen Ollie perform some of David's and Dennis's leads. Though I once heard Richard Street claim in an interview that if you closed your eyes and listened you couldn't tell the difference between Ollie and David Ruffin, I figured Richard must have had twenty years of wax buildup in his ears, because to me, Ollie sounded like an over-dramatic screamer— nothing like the real thing.

Ron Tyson, who sang Eddie's leads, was true to the original, though not a perfect mimic like Eddie's second replacement, Damon Harris. Damon had been thrown out after his once "respectful" attitude disappeared and he started giving Otis some lip, as Otis put it. Worse still, something he said pissed Berry Gordy off, so Berry told Otis to "get rid of him." The perfect opportunity came when Damon cut loose on the mike one night at the Apollo, thanking the audience on behalf of all the Temptations for the expensive minks and flashy cars they helped them buy. That was the end of Damon.

As yet, I didn't know the story of how Otis's group, "The Imitations" as I called them, had threatened to sue Eddie and David for "deceptive and misleading advertising" over the use of the name Temptations. How it could be deceptive or misleading to call two former Temptations "former Temptations," few that I spoke with could ever figure out. But of course, it is very Motown to fight over group names or "service marks," and it is very Motown to control an artist's career and earning power by controlling his name. Let's face it, though: as background singers Otis and Melvin needed the Temptations name far more than did lead singers Eddie, David, or Dennis—all of whom had enjoyed solo careers using their own names.

Motown itself, having apparently forgotten to claim the name "Temptations" when it first signed the group, had later in the sixties secretly applied for ownership of the name, when the Tempts looked like they might be worth something. Otis and Melvin ended up fighting Berry Gordy's Motown machine for the name when they decided to leave the company in 1976, because they knew they were absolutely nothing without it, and Motown finally let them have it. Somewhere in Otis's house hangs a trophy of success, the document transferring rights to the name, framed like a family portrait. How appropriate.

Now, it could be very confusing to have two groups with the same name going out on tour. But in settling out of court, Otis and Melvin insisted that Eddie and David could not in the future call themselves "original lead singers of the Temptations" or "former

Temptations." The most they would finally allow was the billing "formerly of the Temptations," and that was on condition that, as the legal document declared, the letters in the name "Temptations" could never be larger than 25 percent of the size of both the letters used in (Eddie's and David's) individual names, and the letters used in the phrase "formerly of."

Pulling up in the limo at the front door of the Beacon Theater that night in 1989, I immediately caught sight of the name "The Temptations" spelled out in huge letters on the marquee and, in tiny letters that you could just make out, "former lead singers" "Eddie Kendrick, David Ruffin, Dennis Edwards."

I jumped out of the limo, told the security man that I worked for Misters Ruffin, Kendrick, and Edwards, and sailed right into the theater. As I neared the top of the stairs leading to the dressing room, I heard "Tony, is that you?"

"Baby, it's me."

"Get the hell on up here!" Eddie said.

It was just like the old days. We talked about this and that: how Dennis had been fired from the other Tempts once again for being a bad boy; how the three of them had got together after they had met up when they were all inducted into the Rock and Roll Hall Of Fame earlier that year; how they were going to run right through the shadow of the other Temptations; how they had a new management company and they were finally going to make some real money—this time for themselves, they believed.

I told them I was busy writing a book about my adventures with the Supremes, at which David jumped in with, "You've got to tell the truth about that bitch, Diana Ross, and all the rest of them. And Mary was trash. And that Berry Gordy, he stole all my motherfuckin' money."

"That he did, that he did," chimed in an always-understated Eddie.

"And Eddie, tell Tony how Mary chased you all those years."
Eddie blushed.

"That Diana Ross," David went on. "Did I ever tell you about
the time out on one of them old Motown tours, when I pulled the
bitch aside and I said, 'Listen, write the names down of the men
on this tour whose dicks you haven't sucked yet—write that shit
down'?" We all hollered like old school buddies.

Well, the afternoon went on with X-rated story after X-rated
story, until it was time for me to rush back to the apartment, change
my outfit, and take the limo back to the theater for the show.

Scurrying around the dressing room in a fog was someone whom
I knew. It was Judas,* who had introduced himself to me two years
earlier in Chicago as a "Very Good Friend" of Eddie Kendrick's.
He was now apparently road manager of sorts for the former Tempts.
Also in the dressing room was the very striking Margarette, a dead
ringer for the diva Nancy Wilson. She told me that she was now
working with the former Tempts' new management company. Margarette, I remembered from one of the early Motown picnics, had
been a friend of Eddie's and David's and a fan of the Temptations
from way back. It was she who had helped get David into treatment
after Hall and Oates, and who had put the former Tempts together
with the new management company.

Margarette introduced me to Bob, the vice president of the company. Eddie interjected, "Bob, this is the person you should hire
to tour with your clients. He could make their hotel and travel
arrangements and everything." Later that night, when I saw the
fleabag Times Square hotel into which the guys had been booked,
I understood why Eddie wanted the company to hire me. Forget
about the damn roaches—the roaches had to run away from the rats
that were coming out of holes in the walls! Dennis had already
placed his large suitcases in front of the rat holes in his room.

* This name has been changed.

During the course of the evening at the Beacon I learned more about the management company, who up until that time had apparently worked almost exclusively with minor-league, second-string sports figures and were now trying to sign entertainers. They presented themselves as a total management company, the kind that takes you in, handles your earnings, investments, and contract negotiations, pays all your professional and personal bills, and in general babies you by taking every little worry off your delicate, superstar shoulders. They supposedly provided both career and financial services, coupled with commercials and endorsements. I was immediately reminded of Motown.

They had it so beautifully worked out, it sounded perfect. The tone was, "We know you poor, misguided superstars have been robbed. We are legit, and we are well connected. We are here to help you get back on your feet." But looking at Bob standing there looking meek, like an older Pee-wee Herman in his brown polyester pants and his checkered knit polyester sports coat, I wondered how this man was going to help anyone get back on his feet when he couldn't help himself into a decent business suit.

There was hardly time for my suspicions to develop, because suddenly it was show time. I had never seen anything quite like this Temptations show before. It was fabulous, in my opinion the closest thing to an original Temptations show that had been performed in years, except that now there was a female vocalist in the lineup, Miss Josie Short, who had been brought in partly to lend vocal support to Eddie Kendrick by filling in behind his faltering falsetto.

It was like four shows in one—a group show plus solo shows by the three most powerful and individually well-known lead singers of the Temptations. Each of them had enjoyed a substantial solo career, each had a different kind of charisma, each had name power—David Ruffin's name was synonymous with shocking headlines, Eddie Kendrick's meant cuteness and oozing charm, and handsome Dennis Edwards was known for powerful, gospel-style singing. It was a million-dollar formula if I ever saw one. By the time that performance was over, everyone in the audience including myself was exhausted and dripping with sweat.

Hugging them each as they came off the stage, I felt myself hooking onto the chain.

Afterwards I asked the guys, "Who put your new show together? It's unbelievable!"

"Ain't nobody put together this show," Dennis told me. "We didn't have the money for anybody to script, stage, light, and costume the act. We got rehearsal and inexpensive motel space in Detroit and we all just put the show together."

A couple of days later I took the early Metroliner with my new best friend, Margarette, to see the former Tempts perform again in Philadelphia. David's son, David Ruffin, Jr., was on staff, a great big, handsome guy with the body of a football player, who was supposedly working as part of the road crew. Most people thought he was actually doing nothing but getting in everyone's way. So I took it upon myself to put him in charge of security, giving him the job of checking backstage passes and the like, plus following Eddie out into the audience during his solo part of the show in the role of bodyguard.

It seemed as if David just didn't know what to do with his son, and I sensed that although they were close, David Junior wanted to get closer but couldn't. At the time, he was living in Connecticut with his mother, who is white. He was trying to produce some rap singers and hoped to get his father interested in helping him. But David was not interested. Although I thought that David Junior had begun to work hard and take his security position seriously, shortly thereafter he was no longer on the road with his father.

I, however, began to tour with the former Tempts, having jumped right on the chain in the newly created role of "second road manager." Early in July they were working a private, corporate job at a new luxury condominium townhouse development out on Long Island. I arrived from my home in Florida on the day of the show and was driven out to the sound check. It promised to be a beautiful show. The stage was actually a gazebo in the middle of a man-made lake, joined by a long, romantic walkway to the shore. Bleachers had been set up on the other side of the lake for the audience.

Dennis had left his latest wife at home in Dayton, Ohio, and was there with a rather rough-looking New York girlfriend whom I immediately nicknamed the New York Doll. Eddie was there alone, as usual—he rarely mixed business and pleasure—and Bob was there representing the management company. David had not yet arrived. He was supposed to be flying in from Detroit, where he had been staying with his daughter Nedra.

The sound check over, we returned to our nearby hotel and discovered that Ruffin had still not arrived. Judas the road manager had already made two limo trips to the airport to pick him up; he had not been on any of those flights.

Nedra called. She had taken David to the airport, dropped him off outside, and gone home, only to be called to pick him up from a crack house and take him back to the airport for the second flight. She had picked him up, taken him back to the airport, dropped him outside again, gone home, and of course David had disappeared back to the drug den.

By now it was almost show time. The singers and band were ready to make their way from the hotel to the condo site for the performance—all except Dennis, who was still in his room. The New York Doll and Bob were waiting near the elevator for him to come out. I figured the Last Star was running late and was in good hands. As we got into our limos and began to make the short trip to the gig, I caught sight of Bob getting into his Mercedes. Dennis must be with him, I thought.

It wasn't until we were in the dressing room, minutes before show time, that Bob stopped chomping on a piece of barbequed chicken, turned to me, and said, "Tony, where's Dennis?"

His question made my mind flash back suddenly to the moment a few years earlier when Mary Wilson, fifteen minutes into a journey by limo on her big book tour, had turned to one of her devotees and asked, "Where's my mother?" At which the limo driver had informed her that he had noticed an elderly black lady running behind the car several miles back, waving a mink stole over her head. Mother had been left behind. Remembering Mary's response—"Fuck it, I'm late!"—I chuckled to myself, then was jolted back to the present by the realization that not only David but also Dennis was missing, and the show was about to start.

"I left you waiting for him!" I said to Bob. "I thought he came down with you."

"Oh," Bob said. "Dennis never came out. I left because he said he'd be on his way over."

"In what?" I asked him. "We have all the limos here. Dennis was supposed to ride with you!"

The show was intended to be a publicity stunt aimed at bringing qualified, Big Chill Baby Boom buyers to tour the expensive model homes. By now the organizers were milling around us in a frenzy of anticipation, saying "We're ready to start! Put the band on, put the band on!"

Meanwhile, the road manager was making trip number three to the airport, with David's complete stage outfit ready for him to change into in the back of the limo. All we had on hand was the band, the background singers Josie Short and Nate Evans, and Mr. Eddie Kendrick who, unlike Bob, did not panic.

"Oh my God," said Bob.

He called the hotel. Dennis did not answer his phone. The front desk informed Bob that Dennis had not left the hotel. I got on the phone, instructing a reluctant hotel security officer to open Dennis's door. The guy said it was double-locked and probably chained.

I informed Eddie of the latest development.

"Tony," he said, sounding cool as ice, "I have to start. The show must go on. The audience is far enough away that maybe they'll think Nate is David or Dennis. We'll get around it someway. But you get back to the hotel and get Dennis over here quick. I'm depending on you—I know you can do it."

I snatched up Dennis's costume and went racing back with Bob, who knocked on the hotel room door as if it were made of Waterford crystal. "Dennis," he said in a voice that was almost a whisper, "it's Bob."

No answer.

"It's Bob. It's Bob. Dennis, open the door, please."

"Look," I told him, "you have to bang on that door." You could smell the odor of crack coming out of the room. I knew Dennis used crack now and then, but had no idea it had become a problem.

He knocked a little louder. "It's Bob. Let me in, Dennis." Still no answer. "Is something the matter? Let me in."

Bob kept on knocking for what seemed like ten minutes, until I said "Get out of the way, Bob," and I banged on the door like a Supreme locked out of her room without her wig. "Dennis, open this motherfuckin' door. This is Tony, open the goddamn door!"

The door opened a bit. Dennis's face was trembling, his teeth were shifting around in his mouth. "What do you want?" he mumbled.

"Let me in. Eddie is over there doing the whole show by himself, and David is still between here and Detroit—I hope. Now take the chain off and let me in. How could you do this to Eddie?"

"What do you want?"

I forced open the door, breaking the chain, to find Dennis standing there buck naked. The New York Doll was sitting on the edge of the bed with the the crack pipe. I dragged her out of the room, slammed the door, and got to work quickly dressing Dennis

Edwards—underwear, socks, jumpsuit, makeup, hair—doing whatever I could do to make him look totally tempting in a hurry.

As soon as he was ready I guided the Last Star to the door. But before I could get it open and Dennis out, he was stopped cold by his reflection in a full-length mirror. He gazed at himself: "How do I look? How do I look?" Even in this cracked-up state, it was back to the old, firmly ingrained Motown maxim: Appearance is half the game.

"Fine," I told him. "Now, let's go."

"I need more makeup." I added more translucent powder and guided him back to the door. His image in the mirror stopped him again.

"I need more hair sheen." I sprayed his hair heavy and tried to exit once more.

"How do I look? Quick! Put a towel around my neck." I draped a large, white terrycloth bath towel around his neck and told him again, loudly, "Let's go."

We got to the door again. "Oh, no, no. I don't think I look right. I think I should put the collar up."

"Okay, big D, I'll put your collar up and then can we go?"

"Oh, my voice, Tony, my voice. Do I look all right? Am I still looking young? What do you think, Tony?"

To my own surprise, I slapped him across the face and screamed, "Eddie's on that stage, performing alone with Nate and Josie! You look great. Let's go. Hurry!"

"All right, bitch. But I'm not paying for that chain you done broke." And he puffed himself up into his "I will live each and every moment as a star" mode.

I had always thought of Dennis as harmlessly vain—a "pretty boy" as David used to say—but now I was beginning to realize that his vanity was mixed with a strong dose of insecurity.

We arrived back at the show site just as Eddie was doing the closing number, so I never even let Dennis out of the Mercedes. Instead, we headed back to the hotel. Eddie had successfully soloed. Judas was still at La Guardia Airport waiting for David to arrive. This time, Nedra had physically put her father on a plane.

Around midnight, after Eddie had had a huge argument with Dennis, who was now sulking like a spoiled child in his room, David came bouncing in as if everything was just fine.

"Tony," David said, "they better not say shit to me about anything. You got my key? Where's my fuckin' suite—shit!" And he stormed into his room and slammed his door.

Anyone could see that Eddie was pissed—in fact, I'd never seen him as mad—and when Eddie was pissed you didn't talk to him. His icy cool had become a slow but steady, under-the-surface simmer that was likely to boil over any second. As soon as he discovered that David had arrived he wanted to call a meeting. By now, a pattern had been established. Eddie called the shots, Dennis followed his lead, and David did what he wanted, often managing to singlehandedly overturn one of Eddie's "final word" decisions. Only he could do that. This time, David was not coming to any meeting, so there was none.

The next morning Dennis came knocking on my door as if nothing had happened, looking characteristically grand in his gorgeous silk Sulka robe.

"I know everybody's mad at me, baby," he said, laughing. "But Tony, you were something last night! You came in my room when I wasn't doing right and you had the nerve to slap the shit out of me. I told myself, I better not play with this bitch. This bitch done gone crazy!"

He went on, "Wasn't I naked? Did anything happen?"

I knew he was kidding and paid him no mind. Anyway the man was too old for me.

"Sure, you're right," I replied, blowing him a kiss.

"I was out of it. But I knew you wasn't playing and I know how you do when you're furious. You were too much last night. I don't mind you slapping me. Now, come on, baby, give me a hug. I'm gonna be good from now on. It's that bitch who got me all fucked up last night."

He still had the New York Doll in his room. "I've gotta get that girl out of there," he said. "She's a crack addict. She's terrible, terrible. I want you to go in there—I'm going to stay in your room—you go in there and tell that bitch to get the fuck out, and you get her a cab back to the city."

Why he couldn't do it himself, I did not know; maybe he knew that he'd buckle under. I suggested that it would be cheaper sending her to the Long Island Railroad Station instead, and Dennis agreed. Meanwhile, Margarette, who happened to be a drug counselor, called to have a conference with Dennis.

As I was helping the New York Doll pack, Dennis buckled under as expected and decided to let her stay. I went down the hall to see what David was doing. He opened his door and I walked in. The room looked like a cyclone had hit it during the few hours that he had been ensconced there. He quickly started trying out useless excuses on me, complaining about how the airlines had been all fucked up the day before, how Judas had given Nedra the wrong information—"He'll have to go. I want you to take over. I'll have to speak to Eddie about him"—but I knew the real story.

"Did that Dennis Edwards sing my songs?" he asked me.

"Well, when you're not there, somebody's got to sing them." In fact, Dennis hadn't sung anybody's songs. David didn't know yet that Dennis had not made it to the show either. Nate Evans had sung both David's parts and Dennis's. But there would be several times in the near future when Dennis would have no choice but to fill in for David.

"As long as I'm living," David yelled, "I don't want that motherfucker singing lead on my songs. Shit, he uses just as much blow as me. He ain't no better. He's a pretty boy and that's all. What he does isn't even singing, it's just Sunday-going-to-church shouting! Fuck that motherfucker, trying to be me!"

I didn't believe that Dennis ever tried to be David—he didn't have to. And I also knew that behind the vehement words, David was actually growing close to Dennis. They shared the same problem—addiction—and were learning to count on each other for support.

Later that evening I met David's new girlfriend, Diane, who had driven down from Philadelphia in her Lincoln Continental. Right away I could tell that Diane was different. She didn't look like the usual dumb broad groupie type—the type that liked to hang around the Temptations. She seemed very bubbly and outgoing, and I got the sense that, like David's other girlfriends, Diane had some polish. David was attracted to whores, pimps, hustlers, drug dealers, and lowlifes in general. But when it came to his woman, David had always gone for a touch of class.

After the show that night, in the hotel lobby, I introduced David to a friend of mine who was a top Cadillac salesman on Long Island.

"Cadillac Man," David told him, "I want a motherfuckin' Cadillac. You see the color of this carpet? This exact shade of purple? I want a Cadillac with an interior done in this purple color. And I want the outside to be lime rickey green."

"David," I said, "Don't you think that's too loud?"

"Now, you know that ain't loud," he told me. "Baby doll, you remember, I had that Eldorado? I had that leopard skin carpet up in there lining the floor and them leopard skin seats? That bitch was bad!"

"Yeah," I said to David, "and don't forget that other one you had, that stretch limo with the mink interior."

Cadillac Man looked shocked. "A mink interior?"

"Custom, custom, custom," David replied. "Now I'm trying to get conservative. I'm getting too old for some of that shit."

Despite the fact that the first evening's show had been two Temptations short, and despite the fact that David had his usual total shitfit and insisted on being paid his full salary for the night he had not even been there, although he knew that the promoter had cut the money substantially—despite all of these dark shadows and weak links, everything looked bright. The format of the show was incredible. The reviews were very encouraging. It looked as if this new version of the former Temptations—with no real money behind them and no major record company—might finally be on the rise again. It looked like they might even leave the other Tempts lying finished in the mud, despite Motown Records and all the hidden muscle that Otis's group had behind it.

Of course, those old vicious rivalries still linked both groups of Temptations to the past. Otis Williams had dogged Eddie, Dennis, and David to hell in his bitter 1988 memoir, and Eddie, Dennis, and David in turn blamed just about everything that went wrong on Otis. The first thing they would say when there was trouble was, "I bet you Otis and them is behind this." When the group ended up in one city and their entire stage wardrobe in another, Dennis insisted only half-jokingly that once again, Otis was up to his old tricks. "I can see people trying to take our money," he said, "but trying to sabotage our clothes. . . ."

The next show was scheduled for a few weeks away in Philadelphia. Nedra would fly in from Detroit, and although David would now be staying with Diane in Philly, he decided to join the rest of us for the days just before the gig and booked a room at our hotel. We would all be together. I left Long Island feeling that Eddie Kendrick, David Ruffin, and Dennis Edwards, "Formerly of the Temptations," were held together by a chain pulling them, hopefully, in the right direction.

Chapter Eight
White Powder Dreams

The seatbelt sign went out, the captain announced our esti-
mated time of arrival in New York and, watching from my
seat while Florida disappeared below me, all I could think
was, dear God, I hope things don't end up like they did in Philly.

Everyone was buzzing about the upcoming former Temptations'
show at the Ritz, a flashy, trendy club-disco located in the guts of
the old Studio 54 in New York City. I hadn't seen Eddie, David,
or Dennis since that weekend show in Philadelphia two months
before, where they'd sold out six thousand seats, delivered one hell
of a show, and left one hell of an aftermath. I didn't know what to
expect next—believe me, you never really knew. But experience
had taught me to brace myself for the usual unusual.

David was arriving direct from yet another expensive, private
drug rehabilitation center, this one located only blocks from the
Ritz. The center had also been home for Dennis, who had just
finished the same thirty-day rehab course about a week earlier.

Although the bill was in the five figures and this center was reportedly one of the best, I didn't believe you could fully cure a person with a serious addiction in thirty days.

Dennis and David had stayed on in Philadelphia after the show, making the hotel into their home and spending several thousands of dollars on white powder dreams—most if not all of their profits from the show. Not surprisingly, they had ended up in even worse trouble than Eddie. I'd heard that by the time the police broke down the door of David's suite, he had thrown a chair and a nineteen-inch color TV through the window and trashed the entire place, costing himself additional thousands. He'd done crack until he went wild. Objects in the room had begun to move and take on a life of their own.

Dennis was hallucinating, too. But eventually, through his paranoia, he was able to see just what was happening to both of them. He could see what the drugs were doing. He could see the low-life scum surrounding him, the drifters and hangers-on, the drug pushers, the pimps and prostitutes, the suppliers who were being summoned up to the hotel and who were now hovering around Dennis and David like vultures in a feeding frenzy, laughing at them them while they preyed. And through all of this David said that he and Dennis became very afraid of these vicious, dangerous characters.

Everyone else on the staff had left Philadelphia for home. Dennis and David were very much like two little boys whose whole family had left them home alone with an enormous wad of new money, and of course they misbehaved. David finally went berserk just to free himself and Dennis, knowing that if the hotel heard the disturbance they would dial 911, and someone would come and stop him from destroying himself. He couldn't stop himself. Going berserk was David's way of crying for help by making people see that his addiction was out of control.

When help came in the form of the management company, a very overweight Dennis went voluntarily into treatment. David, of

course, insisted that "ain't nothin' wrong with me." The whole episode had been just a binge, he insisted, just a flight of fancy. The
great David Ruffin refused to admit that he was addicted. However
positive he had once felt about drug treatment, when he was in this
drugged-out state the whole idea scared him to hell. And so he fled
to Detroit instead, where he promptly went on another drug binge
and ended up being rushed to the hospital, incontinent among other
things. He also missed checking in with his probation officer—he
was still on probation from a recent indiscretion—and was immediately forced by the court into treatment. The judge put it quite
simply: "Either rehabilitation or jail, Mr. Ruffin."

Good God, we've all got a long way to go, I thought, as I sipped
Dom Pérignon from a bottle I'd smuggled on board. Don't let this
engagement end like the white powder nightmare in Philly.

Well, I arrived in New York and found Dennis to be like a person
totally renewed. He looked great. He was on a diet and had lost a
lot of weight. Dennis was proud of himself, and rightly so. For the
very first time, he talked openly about his previously hush-hush
drug habit: he was singing the praises of rehab, talking about how
very stupid he had been, how many major dollars he had blown.
He talked as if he were out for good. In fact, that's almost all he
could talk and joke about in great detail. Eddie seemed pleased
with and thankful for Dennis's new attitude.

However, when David Ruffin arrived I knew all at once that he
was a seriously ill man. To say that he looked terrible would have
been an understatement. He looked like a vampire on a day pass.
He was reed thin and his skin was utterly ashen and scaly. As we
embraced I wept inside for him, wondering if he knew or believed
in the real love we all had for him.

As they rushed off early the next morning for a live appearance
on the "Regis and Kathie Lee" show in New York, Eddie and Dennis
looked every bit the stars. David, despite a good night's rest and
plenty of cosmetic grooming, still looked slightly unkempt—not at

all like a smooth-singing and -dancing former Temptation, but more like a struggling, has-been star on the comeback trail.

I had called David repeatedly during the previous weeks while he was at the rehab center to talk to him about wardrobe and to make sure he would be properly styled and looking right. I had even set up appointments for manicurists and hair stylists to visit him there. Getting clearance for these visits was no easy matter, for a number of well-known recording artists were hiding away at the facility, ridding themselves of various alcohol and drug habits— David claimed that the center's guests had included Richard Pryor, and the director told me half-jokingly that the people I was sending in to style and manicure David might have to be blindfolded to preserve the confidentiality of the other guests. Looking at David, I figured they must have been. I got out the makeup case and hair preparations, and did the best I could.

The show was a near sellout, another vital smash performance, and the crowd loved them. We seemed to be moving toward the top. The fact that the former Tempts' live performances still had all the glory and magic that they had had in the golden days was their strength; the sadness was that all this other crap kept bringing it down.

The show was spectacular despite the fact that David was so visibly ill, despite the fact that he had to lie down and have oxygen in the dressing room whenever he was offstage. I said to myself, this man can't go on. But the second his ear heard the music and his body felt the music, he hit that stage twirling and doing the splits like he was eighteen again, and his voice, thank God, was in top form.

It seemed like the stage and the applause were another drug for David, as if performing filled the void that at other times was filled by alcohol, cocaine, drugs, or women. He once wrote, "Singing is

a part of my life. Without it I am alone, and that makes me sad."
But as soon as David was back on the road, back in that star
mode, he self-destructed. Something about the roar of the crowd
convinced him he was a demigod, and as a demigod he thought
he was all-powerful—powerful enough to control the white lady
cocaine even though he couldn't keep control over his own life. That
night, when I heard David sing the autobiographical song he had
written when he was eighteen, "Statue of a Fool," to an audience
that was almost down on its knees in front of him, I wondered if
any of those fans knew what was going on inside the great David
Ruffin.

During the performance, almost right smack in the middle, an
older woman barged up to me and demanded, "I must speak to
Eddie Kendrick at once," to which I replied, "Miss, can't you see?
Eddie Kendrick is on stage."

The woman threw back her shoulders haughtily. "I must be taken
backstage. Immediately."

She was in the company of another female, somewhat quieter
but just as old. They were both all dolled up with tons of blatantly
synthetic hair weaved on in the wrong way, and the uppity one had
taken it upon herself not to be just an Eddie Kendrick groupie, but
Eddie Kendrick's sister. I stared at her and knew decisively that
this crass and vulgar woman was probably no sister to anybody, and
especially not to Eddie Kendrick. So I went over to the other road
manager and I told him, "There's a very belligerent older young
lady over there who claims she's Eddie Kendrick's sister. Although
I doubt it, she's demanding to be let backstage."

He told me in no uncertain terms, "Tony, we have a show to
run. You just tell her she'll have to wait."

Now, Judas was in this woman's line of sight. He saw her and
she saw him. I went over and I told her, "The other road manager
agrees with me—you'll have to wait."

"I *won't* be kept waiting!" she screamed. "You'll both be sorry! Do you understand who I am?"

Smiling, I replied, "I'm trying."

She made an attempt to force her way through security while lunging at me, all the while swearing that she was going to get backstage, no matter what I said.

"Fine," I told her. "But let me tell you something. You're gonna wait here until we say you can go up—if and when," I added as I turned to walk away.

"I'll have your jobs for this!" she bellowed.

"Honey, you're quite welcome to have this job," I replied with a smile. "But, my dearest bitch, you can't *do* what I do, therefore you'll never get it." At which I watched her friend gasp.

I had seen these loud and pushy women come and go since I had known the Tempts, and I knew they always would. Now they had the look of has-been Motown teenyboppers, the same hot-to-trot teenyboppers who would chase and surround the Tempts in their early days, the same well-used freaks who back then were trying to look ten years older, and now were in their late forties and all used up, trying to look twenty years younger and still trying to become a Mrs. Temptation, or at least a star-fucker.

After many more vulgar displays of screaming and pushing, the women finally did get up into the guys' dressing room—how, we never found out. The place was already packed full of people giving their congratulations when, in her big, boisterous voice and fake fur coat, the loud one thrust her hands on her flabby hips and shrieked, "Eddie, I don't know who these two motherfuckin' boys are that you have working for you, but you need to fire them because I'm sick of their shit and I want you, Eddie Kendrick, to fire them."

As they sometimes do, the room stood still. You could have heard a pin drop.

Eddie, very elegantly tall and trim, just turned to her and said, "Who are you talking about?"

"That one over there," she said, pointing to me. I was attending to the needs of David Ruffin at the time. "And him," she shouted, spinning around with her fake fur just a-flying, and pointing to Judas. "I want them fired."

Everyone was looking back and forth between Judas and me. Eddie, who never raised his voice or missed a beat, simply looked at her and said, "It'll never happen."

Needless to say, the party continued.

A couple of hours later, back at the hotel, I had an urgent call from Eddie. "Tony," he whispered, "would you please come up here and throw these women out of my room?"

Eddie was always very accommodating to the women who flocked around him—up to a point. In the end, he never seemed that interested in them. It seemed like he would rather spend a quiet evening by himself or with a few friends. So I was always waiting for his calls summoning me to his rescue, and since tonight I knew that these women had latched onto Eddie and followed him back to the hotel, I had been waiting on this call. I knew it would come, and I couldn't wait to get up there, because now I could be a real bitch, now I would have the chance to toss these women out on their fat asses. After all, it was my job as road manager to play the heavy, in order that the star could retain his nice-guy image.

Excusing myself from the crowd in David's suite, I immediately changed into my throwing-her-ass-out outfit—a dramatic raw silk suit and high, fringed suede boots—and dashed to Eddie's suite, where I found both women fully ensconced. Miss Fake Fur and Hair had taken off her shoes, she had her stockingless feet up on the glass-and-chrome coffee table, and she was looking over the room service menu, fixing to order for everyone like she was paying the bills. The other woman had already unbuttoned her blouse. They were in there for the kill.

I smiled. "Mr. Kendrick," I said, looking directly at them, "you're required to attend your staff meeting in five minutes in Dennis's suite."

"Okay," said Eddie. "But I need to talk privately with you first. Just stay with me. It'll only take me a moment to say good-bye to my guests."

"Oh, can't we stay?" asked one of the women, almost begging.

I said, "I don't think so, dear. Our staff meetings go on for hours. I don't think you're the type of ladies, lovely as you both may be, to let the harsh morning light find you in a gentleman's suite. I don't think so, or are you, girls?" Thundermouth didn't try me, nor did her mostly silent partner. They just got up on their too small high heels and left in a hurry.

Eddie shook his head. "Tony," he said, "you're too much."

"But not too soon," I answered.

They didn't know how to be ordinary, everyday people looking after their ordinary, everyday lives. They hadn't been everyday people for decades, since Berry Gordy had put out their first record. They'd had managers, producers, arrangers, chauffeurs, valets, friends, and whores shouting SUPERSTAR at them. Even when they were down, they were still stars, which was probably all they had ever wanted. When Dennis Edwards spent two years away from the Temptations during the seventies, laying driveways for his uncles' company, the other workers would cluster around him and ask for autographs. There was always someone willing to run after them, to pamper them, to claim to understand them, to follow them, buy for them, do or die for them because of who they were, because of who they had been, because their faces were on an album cover. And even now, all they seemed to understand was the show, but not necessarily the business. The show was what they'd lived for since they were kids, except now they were no longer kids living for it, they were middle-aged men living through it.

Long gone were the early days when Eddie, David, or Dennis would jump up if anyone asked them to sing a song, and they would sing for free—when Eddie would lay background tracks in the Hitsville studio for ten dollars, just for the fun of it. Now they were tired and weary and looking for a secure retirement. The clock was ticking. They knew there was scarce possibility of ever again reaching the true, gold-record, million-dollar heights, but they had to go on just in order to survive, in order to keep some ray of hope alive. They realized that at this point in their lives they should not have needed to perform any more. They should have been living the lush life, like Berry Gordy in his Bel Air mansion, playing golf at private country clubs around the world protected by security guards and iron gates.

I remember reading, in his ex-wife's book, about Berry Gordy's past and his life as a pimp to some of Detroit's street whores, way back before he had founded his Motor City dream. Those women were thrilled to hand him their earnings in exchange for the standard pimp's promise: "I'll always take care of you." It was a line that Gordy's clan of Motowners knew only too well from those early days at Hitsville. As a street pimp in Detroit, Gordy hadn't done too well, but as Motown's president he was probably one of the biggest legit pimps in the world. He protected the reputations of his stable of stars, kept them alive and working, and let them know that if they didn't like the way things were, there were plenty more like them out there just waiting to be taken care of. As David was always telling me, "Hell, we're all whores and prostitutes out here." And I thought, how apt—the pimp profits, the whores end up old and used up and fall by the wayside. Whose fault was it?

While Berry Gordy had looked to the long-term, to the business, to his own future, David, Eddie, and Dennis had looked no further than to the night, the show, the drugs, the fuck. And nobody who saw the show now could tell that they were singing for their financial lives, that they were struggling, doing it because it was the only thing they were trained to do, because it was the only thing that kept them from being just ordinary, everyday, middle-aged men with grandchildren and no pension plans. We could only pray that the show would go on, and that they would remain the perfect illusion.

The original Temptations (left to right—David Ruffin, Melvin Franklin, Paul Williams, Otis Williams, and Eddie Kendrick). [© Michael Ochs Archives/Venice, CA]

Berry
Gordy, Jr., the
father of the Motown
family.

The Supremes

Flo Ballard

Mary Wells (front row, center) with Martha and the Vandellas (back row)
[all photos this spread © Michael Ochs Archives/ Venice, CA]

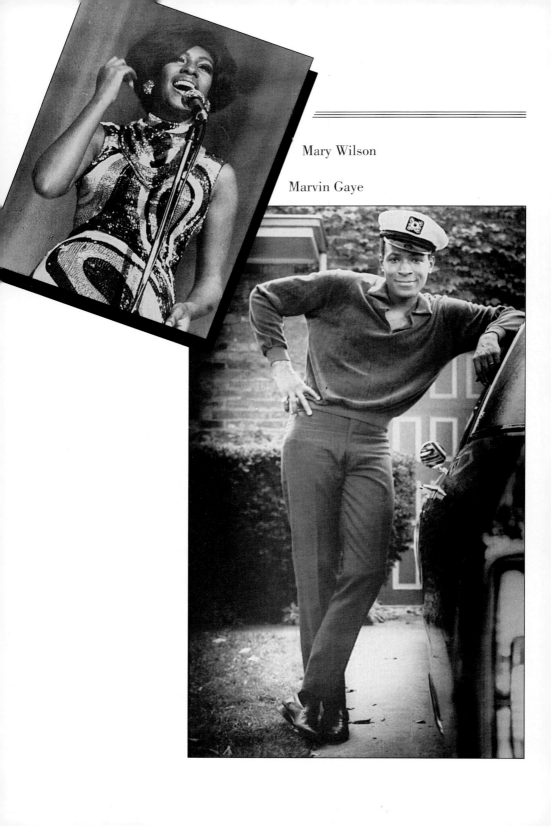

Mary Wilson

Marvin Gaye

Martha and the Vandellas

Aretha Franklin (who wanted
to be part of the Motown
stable, but was spurned
by Gordy)

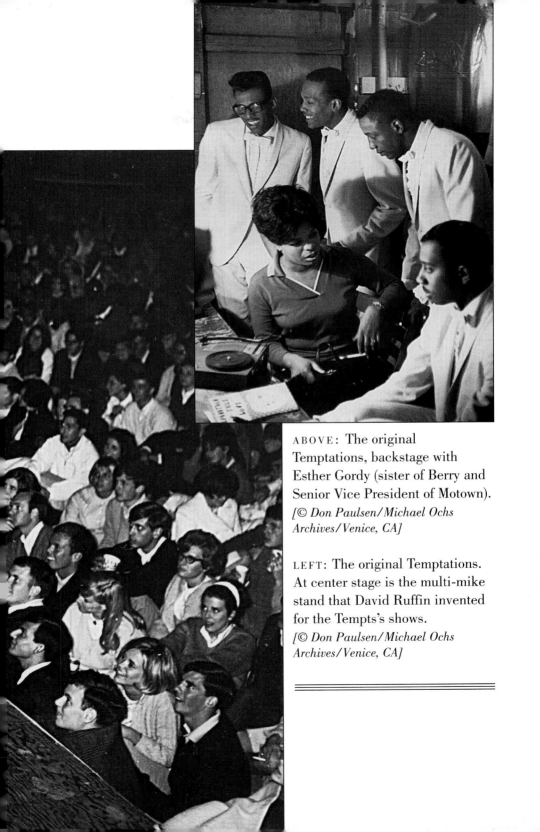

ABOVE: The original
Temptations, backstage with
Esther Gordy (sister of Berry and
Senior Vice President of Motown).
*[© Don Paulsen/Michael Ochs
Archives/Venice, CA]*

LEFT: The original Temptations.
At center stage is the multi-mike
stand that David Ruffin invented
for the Tempts's shows.
*[© Don Paulsen/Michael Ochs
Archives/Venice, CA]*

The Tempts (minus David Ruffin) and the Supremes (minus Flo Ballard) pair up for Motown's first television special in the late 1960s. *[photo courtesy Tony Turner]*

INSET: The Tempts look for a hole in one. *[© Michael Ochs Archives/Venice, CA]*

Keeping in step with the ever-changing lineups of the Temptations:

RIGHT: The original lineup (left to right—Paul, Eddie, David, Melvin, and Otis) *[© Don Paulsen/Michael Ochs Archives/Venice, CA]*

BELOW: Back row—Otis, Richard Street; front row—Dennis, Damon Harris, Melvin *[© Michael Ochs Archives/Venice, CA]*

BELOW: Left to right—Richard Street, Dennis, Melvin, Otis, Glenn Leonard [© *Michael Ochs Archives/Venice, CA]*

BOTTOM: A latter-day incarnation—Otis, Melvin, Ollie, Richard, and Ron Tyson [© *Everett Collection]*

David Ruffin and Eddie Kendrick perform with Hall and Oates at Live Aid.
[© Ken Regan/ Camera 5]

OPPOSITE: Several current and former Temptations get together for the Rock and Roll Hall of Fame induction, 1989.
[© P. Harbron/ Sygma]

LEFT: Eddie, Dennis, and David relax backstage *[photo courtesy Tony Turner]*

RIGHT: Tony and Dennis in Paris, 1991 *[photo courtesy Tony Turner]*

David, Josie Short, Dennis, and Nate *[photo courtesy of Josie Short]*

BELOW: Eddie, 1990 *[photo courtesy of Marguerette Harvel]*

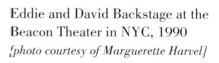

Eddie and David Backstage at the Beacon Theater in NYC, 1990 *[photo courtesy of Marguerette Harvel]*

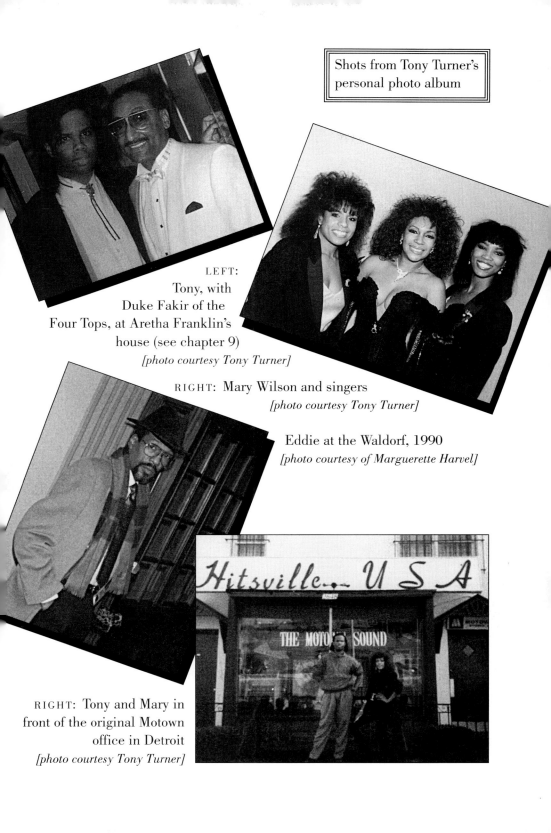

Shots from Tony Turner's personal photo album

LEFT:
Tony, with
Duke Fakir of the
Four Tops, at Aretha Franklin's
house (see chapter 9)
[photo courtesy Tony Turner]

RIGHT: Mary Wilson and singers
[photo courtesy Tony Turner]

Eddie at the Waldorf, 1990
[photo courtesy of Marguerette Harvel]

RIGHT: Tony and Mary in
front of the original Motown
office in Detroit
[photo courtesy Tony Turner]

ABOVE:
David Ruffin's
last photo session, 1990.
[photo courtesy of Diane Showers]

RIGHT: Portrait of Tony Turner in
1992. *[Bill Baker for MLD 111]*

Chapter Nine

Queen of Soul, Our Lady of Perpetual Sorrow

A s always, the show must go on. As we left New York, everyone on staff was excited because we were gearing up to perform the following weekend at a big by-invitation-only party at The Queen of Soul, Aretha Franklin's, mansion in Bloomfield Hills, a very classy Detroit suburb. Robin Leach's "Rich and Famous" crew would be there to film the whole proceedings.

This promised to be an unforgettable event—of that I was sure!

Aretha had personally and especially requested that Dennis, her one-time live-in lover, sing one of her favorite songs at the affair, a song that was Dennis's trademark, Leon Russell's "A Song for You." His interpretation of this number always brought the house down and the crowd to its feet. Dennis had recorded it, and the Queen of Soul herself had also recorded it on her much-acclaimed album, *Let Me in Your Life*. But although we were all in that "ain't too proud to beg" mode and tried hard to persuade him—"Sing it like only you can" we told him, trying to tickle his vanity—Dennis was extremely reluctant to sing "A Song for You" at Aretha's party. He kept saying, "No, I'm not going to sing that song there." It looked like a personal thing to me, almost as if singing that song would be too much of an emotional drain for Dennis at that time and under those circumstances.

Just getting to the party proved to be an event in itself. As usual, David Ruffin missed three or four planes; the man was a travel agent's worst nightmare. I had to keep rebooking his flight arrangements throughout the day. But finally, in shifts, we all arrived at the hotel Aretha had selected for us. It was rumored that she owned it, together with a great deal of prime Detroit real estate.

Rehearsal and sound check were scheduled at Aretha's mansion for one o'clock. Aretha was supposed to be sending limos for us. At 2:30 we were still waiting in the lobby. Eddie was not pleased and Dennis was in an unusually pensive mood. The band, meanwhile, was up and hungry, certain that Aretha would be serving lunch. They had heard that the Queen of Soul did little without food. It was said that in the past she had even taken pots and pans full of her favorite foods into the studio with her.

Finally, up came one limo, a Cadillac that appeared to be dying a dirty death, with a chauffeur who looked like he had just relished the last sip of Gypsy Rose in the bottle.

"ReRe sent this car for y'all," he mumbled. David prayed it could make it back to the house.

So we piled into the limo and rode through lush Bloomfield Hills, past tall, stately trees, high security fences shielding the mansions behind them, big, broad entryways, beautifully manicured lawns, and scenic vistas. Eddie looked like he was silently reminiscing. At his peak, he had lived in this neighborhood. But he had given the house and practically everything else he owned to his wife, Pat, when they divorced in the seventies. I thought to myself, what strength Eddie has! Many would have broken down crying to have had it all and lost it.

I wondered where his mansion had been. "Should we go a bit slower?" I asked. Was it there, around the bend? "Should we slow down?" I was hoping Eddie might point it out, and I longed to ask him to, but I knew Eddie. His private life was his alone, and he had a way of shutting out unwanted eyes. You just didn't ask him questions, however innocent they were—not even his best friends did.

We reached Aretha's mansion in about ten minutes. It was a sprawling, stark white house, a complete extravaganza of contemporary high-tech, the definitive architectural statement on a massive circular drive. If the blue Rolls-Royce missing its hubcaps and the Excalibur had not been there in the driveway, this house would have looked like a square spaceship newly arrived on Earth.

We were welcomed in by Aretha's sister and sometime background singer, Erma Franklin. The first thing I noticed, after the vastness of this home, was a headless mannekin in a glass case, on which was displayed Aretha's Queen of Soul robe. In another case were her Queen of Soul crown and scepter. Aretha herself was apparently in some other region of her house being interviewed for Robin Leach's "Lifestyles of the Rich and Famous."

The house was filled with thousands of dollars worth of fresh flowers—huger-than-you-could-believe displays of gardenias, gladioli, and orchids. Exotic birds sat in golden cages; modern chandeliers hung like amazing glass sculptures from the ceilings. The stark white walls were covered in gold and platinum records, and with photographs of Aretha spanning her whole career. It took me back to the time Mary Wilson moved homes for a day when she was invited to appear on one of Robin Leach's "Rich and Famous" shows. She took all the photographs and gold records off her walls, moved them over to a friend's big old English Tudor mansion, parked her old Rolls-Royce with the Supremes license plate and the ripped-up interior in the driveway, and pretended that this was her house so that nobody would know she was actually washed up and living cooped up with her family in a tiny, two-bedroom bungalow.

But Mary's big production paled by comparison with what was going on at Aretha's. Already, caterers and assistants were scampering about, and everything was in a state of preparation.

"I handled all the arrangements for Aretha," said Erma, already in a party mood at 2:45 in the afternoon. "The place is going to be packed tonight. The Four Tops are coming to hear you guys, and the mayor might stop by too!" People were coming in from all over—from L.A. to New York.

Strategically placed among all the photographs on the walls were several large framed pictures of Dennis Edwards, and of Dennis and Aretha. It was like a shrine to Dennis in there. There were so many pictures that Eddie started kidding him—"Dennis, you didn't tell me you had a house up here in Bloomfield Hills!" Dennis flashed his handsome, boyish grin, but it seemed as if he didn't find the comment the least bit amusing.

"Me and Aretha could have made it," Dennis once told me. "But when you get Aretha you get the Queen's staff and guards. It was like that with Aretha, the times we stayed together. She had her security guards, her hair guy, her makeup guy, her secretary, her assistant, her cook, her this and that, all wanting something from her, and I just got tired of living with all those people constantly in the house."

He told me he was worried that Aretha might be seeking to rekindle an old romance tonight. We all wondered if it would work. Dennis was in a marriage that didn't appear to be a match made in heaven, plus his career was definitely in need of the kind of shot in the arm Aretha could give it. But at what cost? As Berry Gordy once said, "Every form of shelter has its price."

Aretha had all sorts of things planned. Blair Underwood from "L.A. Law" would be there modeling men's furs. Marlena Shaw, the jazz singer, was going to be performing. The fashion show would be upstairs, a reggae band downstairs, and last but not least the former Temptations were going to appear as the stars of the evening.

We went downstairs for sound check to a huge area carpeted in white, and discovered that the sound men were only just beginning to set up the equipment. It was obvious that there wouldn't be time for rehearsal. Eddie's displeasure grew. He seemed very annoyed at something, but nobody was quite sure what, and nobody wanted to ask. I could only assume that he felt he was not being given the full star treatment. He headed us back to the hotel, where we began the process of preparing for the evening ahead.

In the middle of it all my personal manager, Pat, arrived and knocked on my door. "Tony," she said, "there's a man calling for you in the hallway."

"What man?"

She looked stunned and embarrassed. "I don't know, but this man is in the hallway, he's buck naked, he's soaking wet, and he's screaming for you to please get him a razor!"

Looking down the corridor, I told her, "Oh! That's Mr. David Ruffin, my dear."

"That skinny man that I passed in the hallway? That man, dripping wet, standing halfway in and halfway out of his doorway buck naked, who just said, 'Oh, hi,' to me like he was fully dressed? *That* is David Ruffin?"

"Yes. That's what makes him a star," I informed her. "He's eccentric, he's different, he's very daring. He's an international idol. He's my godfather, David Ruffin, and don't look so shocked," I said. "The man is a living legend. He's in the Rock and Roll Hall of Fame. Here, girl, do me a favor and give him this razor!"

The phone rang. It was Eddie, who informed me that he wanted to go to Aretha's, do the show, get paid, and get out. He didn't like the way Aretha Franklin was having things handled so far, and he seemed wary. "I want our whole staff out too. Let everyone know that I said no one is to hang around at Aretha's after the performance."

Rarely was Eddie so firm and determined in his decisions. The staff wasn't thrilled, especially me; we'd had our hopes set on plenty of fun and food. Nevertheless, I had to agree with my boss. The whole setup seemed haphazard, especially coming from a respected performer like Aretha, who should know that sound checks can make or break a show.

We went back to Aretha's and found that the bedroom that had been given the Tempts as a dressing room was everything you might have expected, all laid out with a lavish buffet set on white-and-gold china. As soon as Aretha heard that Dennis, Eddie, and David had arrived, she came knocking on the door as if she were coming backstage at a theater. She looked surprisingly slim and shapely, and was wearing her own hair very short. In her strapless, blue sequined minidress, she looked stunning.

Aretha came in with her hand on her hip, a cigarette dangling from her lips, and some man in tow. Without so much as a small hello to anyone else the Queen of Soul immediately asked Dennis, "Are you singing our song? Did you get my message that I want you to sing 'A Song for You'?"

Dennis told her that they hadn't been able to find the musical charts to it, and Aretha looked a little more than a bit upset. She said she wanted to sing it with him as a duet; perhaps they could do it *a cappella*. But Dennis demurred, saying that his voice wasn't in good enough condition to do it *a cappella*. He was very sorry, he was very gracious, and he was lying. Of course, Aretha didn't know what I later found out—that Dennis had made a vow to a long-time, on-going love interest of his never to sing "A Song for You" specifically for anyone else but her. And I never saw him break his promise. Dennis was nothing if not loyal.

As soon as Aretha's escort turned his back, Dennis whispered to her, "Aretha, now how can you ask me to sing "A Song for You" with your boyfriend standing right there?"

With the boyfriend standing no more than inches away from her, she said, "Honey, this is my house. He do what I say or he can get out."

With that, Dennis introduced Aretha to all assembled. She nodded, then sauntered out of the makeshift dressing room.

As soon as she was out of earshot Eddie said, "I'm telling you, let's do the show and let's get out of here." He told Judas, "Make sure you get the rest of our cash from Aretha's brother, the Reverend Cecil Franklin, before we go on."

Everyone was taking their seats for the show. Despite the fact that the multiple air-conditioning systems required to cool a house this size were going full blast, it was like a sauna in there—that's how many people had been invited to see the former Temptations. Aretha sat down in her Queen of Soul folding chair under a huge picture of her and Dennis Edwards, only about three feet away from where the former Tempts were to perform. She was sitting there very grandly as if she were holding court, with her escort sitting beside her. She motioned for me to come over.

"Baby, what time is the show going to start?"

"Whenever you want it to start," I told her, almost bowing. You felt such reverence in Aretha's presence. She had that knack of making you stand back in awe.

"Well, go on, tell them I'm ready," she said. And then she added, "Don't nobody stand in front of me when the Temptations come out! I want this little area here clear. I want a direct view."

The guys came out in their black jumpsuits and hit the white carpet dancing. They tore Aretha's house down. You could feel the mansion rocking to its concrete-and-steel foundations. They did the full show, with the dance routines and everything, and they did two encores, with the crew from "Lifestyles of the Rich and Famous" filming the whole thing. Aretha stood up and danced most of the

time, and you can bet your mother's bottom dollar that nobody
stepped in front of her. The Temptations, as Aretha referred to
them, were very well received. Dennis personally thanked Aretha,
Aretha said a very few soft words and presented the three of them
with bouquets of long-stemmed red roses, and the show was over.

Or was it?

As soon as Aretha left to watch Blair Underwood model men's
furs upstairs, Eddie instructed me, "Tony, pack up and get all of
our people out of here. Now." David Ruffin, who was sharing a bowl
of chitterlings with me, wanted to stay behind and socialize. But
Eddie was already leaving with some of the band members, and as
he left he told Dennis, "Get David out of here, I don't want him
socializing and getting himself into trouble up here." Then he looked
at me and said, "Tony, I'm telling you, I don't want no foolishness
out of you tonight either. I want everybody, including you, out of
here and back at the hotel within an hour to do payroll. I do not
want my staff staying up here at Aretha's house party—something
is bound to happen."

Big Daddy Eddie the K had spoken, and by this point in time
we all knew that he was the leader. Eddie, once so laid-back, had
taken on the responsibility of holding this whole thing together.
Nevertheless, I couldn't understand his concern. Only in retrospect
did I realize that his ego might be suffering from the fact that he,
Eddie Kendrick, had had to stoop so low as to perform at what was
essentially a house party. Maybe he was also upset by all the attention Aretha was giving Dennis Edwards.

Of course, having to leave didn't please me at all, because I
was ready to see some action. Some of the band members started
complaining about transportation troubles getting back to the
hotel—anything to stay a while longer, eat, drink, and party at
Aretha's. But you couldn't argue with Eddie—unless, of course,
you were David.

Dennis instructed Judas to get the money from Aretha's brother, the Reverend Cecil Franklin. Later, Judas told us that he had found Cecil in a back room with a pile of drugs. Cecil apparently told Judas that he had to go get the money from Aretha, upstairs. As Judas told it, when they got upstairs Cecil kept stalling on the money, started getting evil, and soon enough a quiet argument broke out between them, in the middle of which Aretha appeared. We finally left Aretha's, check in hand, and returned to the hotel thinking the night was now really over.

Not much later, after doing the payroll in Dennis's suite, there came a knock at the door. It was Aretha's sister, Erma. "Dennis, I want to speak to you privately," she said.

We left so they could speak. Eddie went to his room, trailed by a few friends. David and his former personal manager, the "I-shot-Wilson-Pickett-in-the-groin" man, locked themselves in David's room.

The next morning, as I sat eating breakfast with Eddie, in walked Dennis Edwards followed by Aretha wearing a fabulous mink coat and gorgeous high heels. She nodded her head regally, said, "Y'all be sure to come up to the house for brunch," and left.

The second Dennis sat down Eddie and I both asked him, "What in the world has happened now?"

And so the story began, with Dennis telling us how he had been sitting there talking to Aretha's sister the previous evening, and how she had been saying to him that Aretha loved him, and that Aretha had sent her over because Aretha wanted Dennis to go back to the house and spend the weekend with her.

According to Dennis, Erma explained that Aretha wanted to get back together with him. Aretha had seen untold personal disappointments in her life, Erma said, and now felt that she deserved some real happiness. Besides, she added, Aretha could certainly help Dennis's and the Tempts' career.

"You guys could be her opening act," the sister told Dennis. "And you could do a duet with Aretha. Aretha's name would guarantee you a good recording contract and a hit record." She reminded Dennis how rich Aretha was, how powerful, how Aretha owned half of Detroit, she ran Detroit, she'd been done terribly wrong by so many men, she'd always loved Dennis—when suddenly, knock, knock, knock. It was Aretha, bathed in mink and wearing stiletto heels.

Aretha came in saying she wanted Dennis to ride back to her house with her, and Erma left them alone.

"What about your man?" he asked her.

"Honey," she said, "what about him? He knows I came up here to see my man."

"I couldn't believe her," Dennis told us. And we couldn't believe him.

Dennis just told her, "Now Aretha, I'm not with all that. What about this check? Our road managers came back from your place with a check, and we were supposed to be paid the balance in cash."

"Don't worry about that check. I want to get some business straight!" Aretha said.

"Aretha dropped her mink to the floor, and she had nothing else on," Dennis told us. "Man, she was totally nude! No panties, no nothin'."

Eddie and I looked at one another in shock. I'm sure he, like me, was trying to picture the Queen of Soul nude—it could happen! But all I had the nerve to ask was, "What happened?"

"Seriously, nothing happened."

And that was all he wrote. Looking very sternly at me, he added, "But ain't nobody going up to Aretha's for no brunch, or nothing."

Frankly, I knew he knew I wouldn't be pleased at this. I had been getting ready to jump up from the breakfast table and run upstairs to change and race over to Aretha's early to see if I could help Erma with anything.

So it was all decided; we were to return to our homes as scheduled. I called up David, who had not yet appeared, and surprisingly

Aretha's sister, Erma, answered David's phone. It turned out that on leaving Dennis's room the night before, Erma had found David in his room, and had stayed up the rest of the night with him.

I spoke with David by phone because he would not let me into the room, and he informed me in no uncertain terms: "I am not leaving town. I'm staying here in Detroit—tell Dennis to give me the check and I'll get it cashed and send Eddie and Dennis their share of the money."

Hanging up I thought, "Sure, you're right!"

Visions of the aftermath in Philly flashed through my head. I thought about trendy, exclusive drug retreats and rehab programs, and how in David's case the five-figure fee for the thirty days had been wasted.

So we left David with his pipe in the hotel, in the company of Aretha's sister. When he had run up a huge hotel bill and had no money left, he left and headed for the house of one of his ex-girlfriends. She wasn't home, so he broke in.

Someone called the cops, and David was arrested and thrown in jail. The story was all over the local TV and newspapers. Thank God, Aretha made a few strategic calls, a weary David Ruffin was rushed to court represented by a high-powered attorney, and charges were dropped.

That, we thought, was finally the finish of the weekend at Aretha's. Unfortunately, the epilogue came months later when a distraught Aretha Franklin called Dennis Edwards to inform him that her brother and longtime manager, the Reverend Cecil Franklin, had just died, reportedly from a drug overdose. In her time of great emotional stress and bereavement, La Diva Aretha Franklin wanted to warn Dennis, who she hoped would warn others, about the dangers of drugs. She pleaded with him through her tears to be very careful, to stop using them. In her time of need she took time to think about somebody else. She truly was the Queen of Soul, our lady of perpetual sorrow.

Chapter Ten
Isn't It a Shame

1990 was a difficult time, a year of trouble. It was the year that Eddie got way up on his high horse and became really bitchy; it was the year that David got thrown out of the group; and it was the year that I got put out too. It was a year of broken links in the chain that had held us all together through thick and thin, and of escalating tensions between two groups of Tempts whose links had long ago been broken.

Of course, there was nothing new in the animosity between Otis Williams and Eddie Kendrick; a deep hatred had existed between them for years. The way Eddie saw it, the Temptations had always been two separate groups: Otis and Melvin's group, the Distants; and Eddie and Paul's group, the Primes. Those two groups were, to Eddie, like two different species, and as far as he was concerned only one of them was worth listening to. As Otis says Eddie once told him, it was Eddie's view that after he, Paul, and David had left the Temptations, the Temptations should have ceased to exist forever.

So it was no surprise when, in December 1989, our group of former Tempts went to perform in Los Angeles where the other Tempts were living, and Otis and Melvin didn't show their faces for any of the shows. However, Ollie Woodson and Ron Tyson from Otis's group of "Imitations" did show up at one of the performances with a few hangers-on and requisite girls, and from the way they carried on anyone might have thought that the only reason they were there was to steal the show from their arch-rivals.

As the show neared its end, Eddie foolishly but graciously invited Ollie and Ron to join in a number. They jumped up from the audience like two jacks-in-a-box, Ollie thrust his cellular phone into my hands for me to hold, and the two "Imitations" got up on stage, almost pushing the background singers off. Once they were there it seemed like they had forgotten how to get off a stage. They did the entire medley of hits with Eddie, David, and Dennis, and when the medley was over they just stood there, basking in the applause and waiting to join in the closing number.

I kept waiting for them to take their bows and go sit the fuck down. If that didn't happen, I was hoping that Eddie would show them to their seats, or that Ollie's phone would finally ring so I could go drag his skinny butt off the stage. But Eddie didn't say a thing, and nobody called Ollie.

By the time it was all over, Eddie was very annoyed. When he later discovered that Ollie, Ron, and crew had also run up a big food tab for dinners they had ordered in the dressing room, an experienced eye could see that Eddie had become even more furious. But as usual, he hardly said a word to anyone about it; he held it all inside of him together with all the other trying annoyances and disappointments that he had stuffed in there over the years.

Later, we all returned to the hotel, with Ollie and Ron tagging along. During the course of the evening, Dennis asked me to bring some ice to his suite. I went out into the hallway, which was arranged in a U-shape around an atrium, located the ice machine, and just as I had finished pouring the ice into the bucket, I heard all this loud moaning and groaning and carrying on coming from somewhere nearby.

"How embarrassing," I thought to myself as I walked back around to Dennis's suite. I hadn't gone far before I heard the sounds again. Looking around for the source I couldn't see anyone, so I kept walking. I was just coming around the other side of the U when my eyes were drawn across the atrium, to the ice machine alcove in the hallway on the floor below me. I could hardly believe what I was seeing. There, in that tiny ice alcove, the grand Ollie Woodson was making out with some dishwater-blonde white woman whose butt was up against the ice machine! I tried not to laugh out too loud as I raced on down the hallway to give Dennis his ice and tell him what I'd seen.

Later on that night, David called me up and said, "Tony, give me the keys to the car. I need to pick up some things from the all-night drugstore."

Now, nobody really wanted David driving the luxury rental car alone—not only did he have no driver's license and drove like a maniac, the car was leased in Eddie's name. So I quickly came up with some reason for my friend Charles, who sometimes traveled with me, to accompany him. "You don't mind if Charles goes along too, do you?" I asked David. "I need him to get some toiletries for you guys."

I was sound asleep when, what seemed like hours later, Charles came back.

"What took you so long?" I asked him.

"You won't believe it," he answered, looking astonished. I sat straight up in bed.

It seems that David had taken off like a bat out of hell and driven directly and recklessly to one of the worst neighborhoods in

Los Angeles, where he parked outside an all-night drugstore. "I'm going in to get my asthma medication," he told Charles. "You wait here, and then you can go in after I come back. I don't want to leave this car alone around here." It sounded sensible.

Charles waited, and waited, and waited. Finally, he decided that he'd better lock up the car and go check out what was happening with David in the drugstore. He went inside—no David. David had slipped back out through the side door.

Charles made his purchases and was just returning to the car when he saw David rushing up the street.

"Okay," David told him without the briefest explanantion, "get in the car, get in, let's go. Quick. Hurry!"

Well, when Charles told me the story I was sure that David had given him the slip to go in search of a *real* drugstore, which didn't seem like the best recommendation for the drug rehabilitation center he had recently come out of. I started wondering if David, like Eddie, could ever live without drugs of one kind or another.

"I'll bet you if I go and knock on David's door now, I won't get in," I told Charles.

"I'll bet you won't," he agreed.

I decided to try and prove myself wrong.

Even at that time of the morning I didn't need an excuse, so I went down the hall, banged on the door and, sure enough, David didn't answer. Little did I know that this was just a taste of things to come, a short introduction to the strains of 1990—to say nothing of the horrors of 1991.

I had already seen how Eddie, Dennis, and David formed a chain whose individual links gave each of them vocal strength, and a weird personal strength understood only by each other. But now I was starting to see very clearly the inevitable personal tensions in the chain's links; the kind of tensions that result when a group of grown people works together, travels together, plans and misman-ages their futures together, argues, but stays together.

The way I saw things it was this inner tension, more than the too-often reported escalation of egos, that had led to the disintegration of so many groups since the sixties, including the Temptations. And it was probably the same tension that would soon lead at least one of the three former Tempts to think about forging a solo life and career separate from the rest. At the same time, each of the three singers probably recognized that he could not survive as a solo. David had the voice, and a reputation that said, Don't touch; Eddie kept it all together but had very little true voice left; Dennis, with his great voice, blemished reputation, and years of allowing himself to be relegated to the background even while he sung lead, was trapped somewhere in the middle. Professionally, they clearly needed one another.

On a personal level, Eddie appeared to need David more than even he knew because, I was beginning to believe, what he really wanted more than anything was to be able to do all those wild and crazy things David did. Of course he couldn't actually let himself, so it seemed he had to live his life through David. Dennis, meanwhile, had always needed someone to follow, and in their own ways, Eddie and David provided the leads for him. And David—perhaps David needed Dennis and Eddie to take the edge of that terrible feeling of loneliness that seemed to pervade his life.

Sometimes I wondered if David's chronic irresponsibility to the group, and especially to himself, might have something to do with these tensions. Maybe he felt torn by his opposing needs to stay true to himself by pulling away, and yet to stay linked. Ever since I knew David, he'd been struggling to maintain his individual identity, whether it meant wearing cowboy boots when everyone else was wearing dress shoes, or lining his car with mink, or not showing up for an engagement because he'd decided that the contract was no good, or the promoter was out to rip them off. Eddie and Dennis would be waiting for him to show up for a sound check, and he'd be sitting at home, thinking, They know why I'm not there. I told them not to do this one. After ten years of battling Motown's stranglehold over his life and career, David was struggling for control.

I started to understand all this about three weeks after the California tour, when the three former Tempts were in Indianapolis to do a couple of New Year's Eve performances at the Indiana Roof Ballroom, next door to the Embassy Suites Hotel where we were staying. It started out in a highly typical fashion. The singers were booked on connecting flights through Detroit from Florida, but when they got to Detroit they discovered that they were in for a long layover in the first-class lounge because of bad weather conditions. David decided to leave the airport. Even ass-deep Detroit snow was no threat to him. Some time later, when the flight was ready to take off, David had not yet returned.

Everybody but David arrived in Indianapolis, did the sound check, and prepared for the show. David was still drifting around somewhere in Detroit. Dennis's wife, Beverly, had driven through the cold from their home in Dayton, Ohio. Dennis, as usual when she was in tow, was busy walking on eggshells and acting like a scared little boy, trying to keep his on-the-road secrets from Big Mama. Meanwhile, Eddie was quietly simmering.

By the time David finally showed up, Eddie and Dennis were already up on stage and halfway through the first show. As instructed by Eddie, I had David's stage costume all ready for him in the dressing room, which was on a balcony level overlooking the main ballroom. The moment he walked in I immediately started trying to get him ready so he could get up on the stage before midnight. But David was in no hurry. He acted like he had all the time in the world, engaging me in idle and sometimes incoherent chit-chat. Meanwhile, I was listening with the other ear to what was happening on stage below us, and I could hear the show steadily speeding by.

I was still trying to get David to put on his socks when he

announced, as if it were an everyday thing, "Oh, by the way, I'm going solo."

"When are you going solo?" I dared to ask him.

"I'm going solo to-motherfuckin'-night. What's wrong with you, bitch? Are you crazy?"

I stopped trying to maneuver David's feet into his socks. "You're going solo tonight?"

"That's damn straight," he said, "I'm sick of this group shit. I got to be here, got to do this, and you all got clothes waiting on me to wear. I don't want to wear this shit tonight. I want to wear what I want to wear. But now I've got to wear this because I'm in a group. I'm sick of it. I'm going solo, and you're going with me. Fuck that cheapskate Eddie."

He went on and on. I just figured it was the drugs and his weariness talking so I paid him no mind and finished getting him ready. We came out of the dressing room and onto the main balcony area, where some of the audience was eating and drinking, watching people dancing in the ballroom below. From there we had to descend a long, narrow spiral staircase to the stage. We inched our way down, with David scarcely able to negotiate the tricky metal steps while he continued screaming at me in full hearing of everybody there about how he was going solo, he was putting his own band together, he'd had enough of this shit, and on and on while the minutes ticked by toward midnight and 1990.

When we finally reached the stage area I begged David, "Just rush onto the stage, because it'll soon be midnight, you know, and everybody's going to expect you to be included in the 'Happy New Year' festivities and all that."

"Fuck you!" he screamed. "Don't you *ever* tell *me* when to go on stage, you motherfuckin' taskmaster diva bitch. I've been in show business as long as you've been living and wearing makeup, and I know exactly when to hit that stage. Don't you understand that everything is a matter of timing? I must feel the moment—surely you understand that by now, bitch. You know me, baby. You and me can bring in our happy new year right here, because I'm going on the stage after midnight. I'm going on in 1990!"

I knew from experience to stand there quietly and just wait for David to go on. But he didn't. At half a minute before midnight Eddie and Dennis stopped the show and began the countdown; David didn't make a move. I thought it would be perfect timing for him to make his grand entrance at the stroke of midnight, but that passed and he was still standing there in a corner. As they broke into "Auld Lang Syne," David came over, hugged me, gave me a big kiss, and said, "Tony, get me one of those desserts from those waiters."

David finished his gourmet dessert as the first show came to a close. The background singers moved to the front of the stage with Eddie and Dennis, joined hands in a chain, and raised them for a final bow. This was the exact moment David chose to drop his plate and dash up onto the stage, break into the chain of hands, and take a bow with them. David, as usual, had been right; timing was everything. The crowd went wild. But Eddie wasn't pleased at all. He snatched his hand away abruptly from David and left the stage. Dennis saw Eddie leaving and followed after him, while David launched right into what he believed to be the start of his solo career.

I had to race after Eddie and Dennis, who were quickly making their way up the spiral staircase to the dressing room. Once there, Eddie immediately started stripping off his clothes like a wild man in heat and changing into his after-show outfit. "Tony, keep your motherfucking godfather away from me. I don't want to be bothered with him tonight. I'm going up to my suite." I hadn't seen Eddie so visibly angry in a long time. It must have driven him crazy to see David so singlemindedly fuck things up for him, and then go out and charm the crowd to death like only David could do.

Dennis shook his head at David's antics and said, "Can you believe it?" He didn't give it any energy.

I raced back down the staircase, almost killing myself, to be ready for Mr. Ruffin when he completed his impromptu show.

"I know Eddie and Dennis are mad at me," he said as he left the stage, "but I've had it with them. I'm going solo. I've done *gone* solo—shit!"

I knew by now that, if you were smart, you never took sides when Eddie and David were at odds with each other. That was unwritten rule number one. If you did take sides, you'd never last. So I kept Eddie and David out of each other's way between shows that New Year's Eve. When it was time for the second show, David once again waited in the dressing room, this time complaining about shortness of breath. And once again, when the show was just about over, he bounced up onto the stage and proceeded to give a twenty-five minute solo performance to an enthusiastic audience while we all waited to see what Eddie would do when we got back upstairs to our hotel suites. I was prepared for a big chill to set in between Eddie and David, just as it had set in outside, where the frigid air was almost unbearable.

Despite the cold, David walked into the hotel suite after his solo show looking quite tropical in a pair of brown bermuda shorts, suede slip-on shoes, gold jewelry, and a gold silk shirt. He had ordered champagne and hors d'oeuvres for everybody on staff and, having greeted the assortment of fans that had followed us upstairs, got set to make himself the toast of the party.

We staff members were still expecting the worst, so there was a moment of definite but not shocked surprise when David put his arms around Eddie. Eddie wished him a happy new year, and suddenly all was right with the world. By breakfast the next morning, everybody knew that David was surely not going out as a solo act, and that everything would remain just as it had always been—Eddie and David, a friendship impenetrable to outsiders and linked in steel, with Dennis, forever looking like the handsome usher at the wedding, traipsing along behind them and wondering what was going to happen next.

It was 1990. A new decade had begun and nobody knew or understood what it would bring.

Soon after came one of the strangest episodes of my life with the Temptations; an episode that, once again, revolved around the great David Ruffin.

David had for some reason always been very protective of me and had never let me see him actually using drugs, which was why it came as something of a shock the first time I ever saw him openly doing cocaine. It seemed like he just didn't care anymore. He didn't want to, or couldn't, stop and hide everything just because I came in the room.

It was February 1990 in Baltimore, Maryland, where David, Eddie, and Dennis were booked for a few shows at the Civic Center. We were all on the same floor at the hotel, except Eddie, who was in his not-speaking mode and had insisted on being separate and taking a room on a floor somewhere above us. I thought this was wise since the goings on in our hallway were like a condominium full of newsy and nosy neighbors. Everybody knew pretty much what everybody else was up to—anyway, Dennis didn't even try to hide the fact that he had made a drug connection as soon as he had arrived at the hotel: one of the guys who worked on the hotel staff was providing a little more than standard room service. His supplementary menu included take-out soul food from a nearby restaurant, which my friend Charles, Josie Short, and I were taking advantage of, and for the more selective palate, cocaine. Dennis opted for the full menu.

Dennis started doing crack until, at the end of the first night, he decided that the guy was ripping him off. "He just gave me a good price to get me started, and now he wants more money and he's bringing me less, that little black bastard," Dennis told me indignantly.

"Have you ever!" I replied, taking another bite of barbeque ribs.

I was never aware of Mr. Room Service knocking on David's door. But when David called me to his hotel room on that first day in Baltimore I found him sitting there with his crack pipe and a plastic bag full of white rocks, all laid out in full view of anyone who cared to see. David looked terribly ill. He couldn't breathe too well, he was wheezing with asthma, and his face was ashen. Between hits on the pipe he would give himself hits on his asthma inhaler, until finally it seemed like the inhaler just wasn't enough. Margarette, who was there for the show and understood his condition better than anyone, decided it was time to take David to the hospital.

At first David resisted vehemently, but after barely making it through the first night's performances and then staying up doing crack until he couldn't breathe again, he finally gave in and let Margarette take him to the emergency room at around three in the morning. I kept Eddie informed of what was going on.

Margarette sat in the hospital the rest of the night and half the next day, while the doctors gave David oxygen and tried to find his veins so they could shoot him up with much-needed medications. They said he was in such bad condition that he was at risk of dying at any moment, and wanted to rush him straight to the intensive care unit. But David would not hear of it. He left the hospital with Margarette, got back to the hotel, picked up his crack pipe, and by late that afternoon was unable to breathe again.

Margarette rushed David back to the hospital, where they insisted on admitting him to intensive care. Around seven o'clock, David— who had drips attached to his arms and was hooked up to oxygen —told the doctor, "I'm leaving. I've got a show to do. People are waiting to hear me. If I don't appear, they'll be let down."

"What kind of a show could you do, Mr. Ruffin?" the doctor asked him. "It takes two people to hold you up!"

"Listen," David told him, "if I don't do the show we won't get paid. I've got fourteen families depending on me." He promised to return so that the doctors could stabilize his condition enough to keep him alive until he got back to Detroit.

Margarette rushed him back to the Civic Center with a police escort and set up a private room for him with oxygen ready in case he should need it. I helped him into the dressing room, dressed him, and held him up in the wings with Margarette's help. We were all scared he was going to die right then and there, but the second they announced his name he broke away from us, leapt out onto the stage, and as he became visible to the audience he did a series of Michael Jackson–style full spins, landed in a James Brown split, threw his microphone up in the air, caught it, and launched into the song. It was totally Ruffin.

While the capacity crowd leapt to its feet in mass approval, we stood in the wings with our mouths hanging open. Where was this strength coming from? He performed beautifully. He kept going through the entire show, and the split second he was offstage and out of view of the audience, he fell back into our arms.

After he had been back to the hospital and checked himself out again very early in the morning, David called me to his hotel room. I arrived to find him seated on the toilet, naked.

"Okay, Tony" he said. "Listen, baby doll, I don't want anybody near my room tonight. I'm dying. I know it—it's too late. You can't walk me, you can't give me coffee, you can't give me a cold shower. I'm dying tonight and no one can help me. Take all of my drugs, the pipe, the whole pack of this shit—take everything, throw it in the garbage, put it on another floor, let someone get in a cab with it and drive twenty miles, dump it out, and come on back. But don't come to my room before ten o'clock this morning. I'm going to be dead in the bed."

I wanted to call for a doctor. Margarette wanted to rush him back to the hospital. But David was adamant. "Clean this room and straighten it up, because the police are going to be all over here. I'll be dead by sunrise."

Who was I to argue with him? Anyone could have easily held him down and called the ambulance—he was so weak he couldn't have fought a six-year-old child. But I didn't call the ambulance and nor did anyone else. I followed what I felt were his last wishes, and did what he asked of me. I took instructions from a man who had been doing drugs and hitting the pipe for years, and all day that day, and all day the day before. We were all under his spell, caught in his nightmare. And he was telling us he wanted to die.

I believe that David felt he was dead already—he just hadn't fallen over yet. He realized what he had done to his body. He realized what he had done to his life. He'd had everything he wanted—women, money, drugs, cars, applause—but he had failed. Inside himself he knew he had only himself to blame.

Aimlessly, mechanically, I cleaned his room and fixed his clothes while someone else got rid of the drugs so that everything would be clean the next day and it might be said that David Ruffin was found dead in his bed, cause unknown. It was as if we were doing him a favor, just like Cleopatra's faithful handmaidens had prepared her tomb and assisted her in her own death. We left him and went back to our rooms.

I called Eddie, who was upstairs in his room and staying well out of the whole mess. He didn't want any part of it. He told me, "Tony, you just better take care of him and his shit. From now on you work just for him." Clearly, Eddie didn't believe that Ruffin was on his way out. "You just get him to the stage on time and in shape. I don't care how you do it. He's your responsibility." Suddenly I had a new position—baby-sitter.

Dennis was in his room across the hall, oblivious to David's pain. The rest of us held a vigil, sitting up all night talking to one another, wondering what stage of death David was at. We left our doors open to the hotel corridor so that we would hear if David called out for help. But all was quiet. We sat and waited, talking about nothing.

We waited until morning came, until people started to move around the hotel, and only then did we decide to go check up on David Ruffin. Apprehensively, I knocked on his door. No answer. I knocked again. My heart started racing. I banged on the door. Still no answer. In a complete panic unlike anything I had experienced, I rushed down to the front desk to get a second key to the door. The lobby was packed with guests checking out. Frantically, I forced my way past them, interrupted the desk clerk, and demanded a key for Mr. David Ruffin's room.

"If you want a key," she said, "you should get it from Mr. Ruffin. He's in the coffee shop."

Sure enough, there was David enjoying a continental breakfast. He had apparently forgotten everything that had happened the night before. When we went back up to his room he immediately started looking for his drugs, to no avail. "Where's my shit, Tony?" he screamed at me, as if I had stolen and consumed his entire stash.

A week later, we were supposed to appear on a double bill with the Four Tops at the Riverside Theater in Milwaukee. It never ceased to amaze me that the fabulous, original Four Tops had stuck together all those years, completely untouched by scandal. I couldn't think of any other Motown group you could say that about. I wondered if maybe the Tops had survived the Motown system because, when they joined the company in 1963, they were older guys already well established on the Detroit scene, and not so impressionable.

David had not shown up for the previous two performances in Madison, Wisconsin, and when he didn't show in Milwaukee we wondered what we were going to tell the Four Tops, because we knew that they were booked for a huge tour of forty or so cities, and we knew that they were considering taking us on the road with them. In fact, from what we had heard, there was an 80–20 chance that we would get the job instead of Otis's Temptations. Once again, the competition was fierce.

Around four o'clock the Four Tops showed up, and luckily they gave us no time to make any excuses for David. The first thing lead singer Levi Stubbs said was, "We know David's not here."

"How do you know?" Dennis asked.

"Because we just seen him in Detroit. We were in our limo, coming through the city on our way to the airport, and we saw him scrambling for crack out on the corner. We think he was selling his Rolex. We had the driver pull over, and we said, 'David, come on, what are you doing? You've got a show to do tonight.' He told us, 'Oh, I'll be there. Go on and I'll be there later. Tony's going to get me my ticket.' Well, we told him to fly out with us, we told him we could get him a ticket and everything. But he wouldn't come with us."

They knew David as well as we did, and they knew he would never make it. Eddie and Dennis went on and performed by themselves, opening the night's concert for the Four Tops, and the Tops took Otis's Temptations on tour with them. It was the last straw for Eddie Kendrick, though he never said anything at the time—he just clammed up. Next thing we knew, David was out of the group. This is how it happened: David received a call in Philadelphia from the management company telling him he was fired. He immediately told Diane, who immediately called the company back to ask them, "How can you fire David?" At which they replied that *they* were not firing David—Eddie had called them and told them to fire him. And that was that, though nobody would believe it for some time.

Later on that day I was standing nearby while the Four Tops' tour bus was being loaded, when I noticed in the luggage compartment several crates of cough medicine. I was intrigued.

"They've got a lot of cough medicine on that bus!" I commented
to Dennis later.

"They're hooked on Robitussin!" he joked. "That's why they're
so mellow. It's a cheap high."

Our next engagement was in April at Sweetwater's, a lively New
York soul club. In place of David, Eddie had decided to add another
singer to the background—a great undiscovered soloist by the name
of David Sea. Although David Ruffin was not with us, his girlfriend,
Diane, had driven up from Philadelphia for the show. She said
David was doing fine. He was gaining weight and sleeping a lot,
building up his strength so that he could get started on some songwriting, and maybe even some recording.

"Eddie," she said, "you should hear him. He sounds great!"
But Eddie was not about to take David back. In fact, as I discovered
later when I went to get my pay, we were both out in the cold.

"The guys are trying to cut back," Judas told me. "As you know,
Tony, they don't have much work coming in now that we don't have
Ruffin with us anymore—and you know he was supposed to be your
responsibility. Also, their pay's been cut almost in half, so the guys
say they can't keep you on the road any more. You're fired."

Eddie never, ever said a word to me about it, and neither did
Dennis Edwards. But I was certain that the large bonus included
in my usual salary must have been Dennis's idea. He was always
as generous as Eddie was cheap.

David pretty much stayed at home with Diane for a while after
he was out of the group. At first he was depressed. He slept a lot.
Diane took excellent care of him, nourishing his body and spirit,
and sheltering him. She fed him, bought him clothes, sat with him
at night, and when he started working on a solo album, she went
with him to the studio.

I would call him at night every other day and chat with him.
When I told him that I was no longer with Eddie, he said, "Isn't it
a shame that sometimes the road must end. Not to worry, Tony.

You still got your godfather." Another time he told me, "Tony, Eddie firing us was the best thing that could have happened. Find me work. Let's regroup and hit the stage again."

As time went by, David's old weaknesses began to creep back up on him. Diane would let him take her car out and he would disappear. She would go out into the night, find a cab, roam the back streets of Philly till she found him in some hellhole, and take him back home.

One night Diane got a call from the police: "Do you know a Mr. David Ruffin? Claims he's a Temptation?"

"Yes," she told them, "and he is most definitely David Ruffin of the Temptations."

"Well, we have a fourteen-year-old down here that has your Lincoln Continental and a signed piece of paper saying he bought it from a Mr. David Ruffin for twenty dollars." David had traded the Lincoln for twenty dollars worth of crack. Diane went and retrieved her car, begging the police to keep the story out of the papers.

The story reminded me of another unorthodox trade David had once made. He had come back to the farm after a stint in a Detroit crack house, trailed by two young boys about eight and ten years old. It turned out he'd bought these two children from some woman in a drug house, because she was trying to sell them for crack money and David was scared that something bad might happen to them. People told him, "You can't buy children!" But David never cared about the rules; what counted in the end was what was in your heart. He had a great time playing Pop for about a week, and then he managed to track down the kids' aunt and turn them over to her.

David by now weighed a little over a hundred pounds. He was like a walking skeleton, and Diane began to talk about trying to commit him to a drug program where he could spend at least two years straightening out. But he would not go into treatment voluntarily.

"I ain't going into no fuckin' program," he told me. "Do you know how much money that costs? Nobody's going to pay that for me, and I've got no medical coverage. You and Diane are not being realistic. You're right, I need to be in an exclusive sanitorium, a fucking Beverly Hills nuthouse where I could get myself straight. But I don't have the money because I've been robbed all my life. Don't nobody care shit about me. Not even my Eddie."

"Oh no, we care about you. We just don't know what to do."

"Leave me the fuck alone." That was his attitude. I didn't know that David had been forced to drop out of drug treatment for lack of funds the last time he'd been admitted. Back home at the farm, he'd called all over the place trying unsuccessfully to get himself into different programs. In the end he joined up with the local chapter of Alcoholics Anonymous but he couldn't get much help there because this was the countryside, and these people had hardly even heard of crack. Hearing about this, I started to understand David's bitterness toward a system that spends thousands of dollars jailing the addicts that couldn't afford to get help.

Around August I came up with a solo booking for David performing for the tenth anniversary of a big law firm in Florida. We were billing him as "David Ruffin, the Voice of the Temptations." Eddie and Dennis's band had already agreed to work with him on any engagements I came up with; and since jobs had been sketchy for the former Tempts since David had been thrown out, there wasn't much risk of double-booking.

As God would have it, between that time and November everything changed. Eddie and Dennis got a major, three-week booking at the Sands Hotel in Las Vegas. As they left for that engagement, they discovered that Nate Evans, one of the background singers, suddenly couldn't make the engagement for personal reasons.

Eddie panicked. He went completely hysterical. The lineup was suddenly one person short. "It won't work. It won't work," Eddie kept on saying. No one could figure out why it wouldn't work. Maybe it had suddenly occured to Eddie that he was about to do three weeks at the Sands Hotel, and he had no David, no "Voice of the Temptations," to give the group its strength. Anyway, Eddie decided to call Diane in Philadelphia and tell her to put David on the very next flight to Vegas.

David rushed off to Vegas. He was back in the group! Three days later Nate got his whole situation cleared up—it had all been a big misunderstanding—and then there were six. David, who I heard was looking thinner and sicker than ever, spent his nights wandering up and down the Vegas strip with a string of various drug dealers. When it came time to leave, he stayed in Vegas, went on a big drug binge, and ran up a huge hotel bill as usual. The whole engagement ended up being extremely problematic.

Nevertheless, David was once again one of the former Temptations. Less than a week before his engagement in Florida, he called me.

"How you doin', baby doll?"

"I'm doing fine," I told him. "I heard there was some trouble out there in Vegas."

"Well, I'm back now and you will be too soon. I'm going to Japan."

I said, "When are you going to Japan?"

He hesitated. "Well," he said, "you know, I'm back, I'm back, baby. They need me, baby. I am back."

"Oh, that's good."

"Yeah. I'm going to take care of everything—you're gonna be back too. You're coming back. Yeah." Pause. "We're going to Japan."

"Well, we have this job on Saturday," I reminded him.

"Oh baby, fuck it. You know I'm gonna make it. I told them motherfuckers, I told them 'you've got to get me down to Florida on Saturday, because I got a solo show to do.' I told them, 'Tony has me booked as a headlining solo, motherfucker'."

So now I had David and the band arriving from Japan at five o'clock if all went well, for an eight forty-five show, with a sound check—which they would surely miss—scheduled for two o'clock. It was tight, but it was certainly possible. Why I decided to be honest and call the promoter to tell him the situation, I don't know. The promoter threw a fit, canceled the show, and demanded all of the deposit money back.

In the midst of all this a call came into my office from two men in Philadelphia.

"Hello, Tony Turner?"

"Yes? Who is it?"

"This is Butch." He introduced another man who was on an extension with him. "Tony, we just spoke to Mr. Ruffin in Japan. We're Mr. Ruffin's managers. He said you would be handling him for the Fontainebleau Hotel engagement in Miami."

"Yes." I knew at once that these two men had nothing to do with the management company. I wondered who they were.

"David wants you to have a limo pick us up. We're coming down for the show. And Mr. Ruffin said you are to have a hotel suite booked and ready for us. We like to travel with him at all times."

"Well, why aren't you in Japan with Mr. Ruffin, then?" I asked.

"That's neither here nor there. Mr. Ruffin wants these arrangements made."

I said, "Sure, you're right," and I hung up the phone. I didn't even call David.

I was still dealing with the irrational promoter. I told him he couldn't legally ask for his money back, because there had been no breach of contract. He said there was no way David could make it on time. I assured him there was no problem. It went back and forth, and in the thick of it all my office received another call.

"Tony, have you made the arrangements as Mr. Ruffin asked?"

I told Butch that I hadn't spoken to David, and that they might as well hold their plans because it looked like David's solo show in Florida wasn't going to happen.

"Well, when we spoke to Mr. Ruffin in Japan he told us there was some disturbance, but he assured us it would all be taken care of and that you were to go ahead and make those arrangements." And he proceeded to give me their flight number.

The attorneys from the law firm who had hired David were threatening to sue David Ruffin because they had been planning their tenth anniversary event for about two years and they had spent the last four months expecting "The Voice of the Temptations" to perform.

Butch called again. I told him the show was definitely canceled and not to come. But it wasn't the last I heard of him. During the afternoon of the Saturday on which it had been scheduled I got a call at my home.

"Hello, Tony?"

"Yes?"

"This is Butch. Where's everybody at? Me and my partner are down here in the Fountainebleau Hotel lobby."

"I told you it was canceled and not to come."

"Well, we decided to come anyway. You had no limousine waiting for us."

"Well, isn't that special."

I slammed the phone down in his ear.

A few days later David called me from Philadelphia. I asked him about Japan.

"Oh, it was a fuckin' mess," he said. "Eddie was in the bitchiest mood ever. He wanted us to spend nine thousand dollars apiece on some new stage outfits, or 'uniforms' as he calls them. I told him I didn't want to spend that kind of money. So we had a big argument, and I think Eddie ended up ordering some anyway."

"You know, Tony," David went on, "Eddie was acting very

fucked up and pissed off the whole time. I don't know what's the matter with him. You know, you're always worrying about my health—I'm telling you, you better check up on Eddie. He cursed out the promoter, he cursed out Dennis—of course, he didn't curse me out, baby, but it was all a big shambles. Tony," he said, "I'm going to get you back on the road with us."

I said good-bye and hung up the phone.

1990 was almost over.

Chapter Eleven

You Are Very Motown If . . .

avid had been out of the group for about eight months when Eddie panicked about Vegas and took him back again. Bookings had dried up considerably without David Ruffin, because he was seen by most promoters as the group's main draw. Eddie had been showing signs of strain. It couldn't have felt too good to him or his ego to be so dependent on David for getting work. He was in danger of becoming another Otis, living off other people's voices and his own reputation for reliability.

Of course, Eddie always took David back. They were like brothers or soulmates who loved and hated each other. It was a deep relationship, and everybody on the inside knew that no matter how badly one hurt the other, they would always be able to overcome it because David had a great big heart, and Eddie had lots of common sense.

David had been back with the group a month or so when he called me at my home in Florida.

"Tony, we're coming down to Tampa. What's happening in Tampa, Florida, baby boy?"

"Really?" I said. "You're doing a show down here?"

"We're doing the Super Bowl," he told me. "We're doing the Super Bowl half-time show with New Kids on the Block."

They had beaten out Otis's Temptations for the job and he was very excited. "It's going to be seen on TV by millions of people. It's going to be satellited around the world. It's going to be seen by our troops in the Gulf, the whole bit. It's a big thing, and I'm going to want you to be there with us, because I don't like the way things are going on the road. "Judas is no road manager."

I pointed out that being road manager was a hard job for someone with very little experience and, given that David, Eddie, and Dennis were three stars who were used to functioning individually, they really needed a well-rounded personal assistant each, plus one well-trained head road manager.

"Well," David told me, "I think you should come back to work exclusively for Dennis and myself as our personal assistant. I'll speak to Eddie and Dennis about it. But I don't care what Eddie says. He can't carry the show without me and Dennis."

Then he said, "You know how cheap Eddie is. Eddie's going to hit the ceiling about the money situation, so Dennis and I will be responsible for your salary and traveling expenses. If Eddie wants to keep hanging onto his boy, he can pay him out of his pocket."

I was on the phone almost daily with David, seeing how things were shaping up or just to say hello. One time, soon after our Super Bowl conversation, he called wanting some information about housing costs in Tampa because he was looking to relocate either there or to Las Vegas. Now that he was back working, he was determined to put his money to good use. He sounded very positive.

By now, the sports world was talking about nothing but Super Bowl, Super Bowl, Super Bowl. Tampa was planting palm trees like crazy, lining the highways with these tall, exotic, tropical things.

The city was in high gear. Crews were all over, cleaning and scouring. There were several huge parades planned. The hotels were booked solid, and every place had "Help Wanted" signs out. Tampa was about to become part of Super Bowl history.

Eddie, David, and Dennis—the Three Stooges, as I'd started calling them—were arriving about four days ahead of time for intensive rehearsals. They would be staying on exclusive, trendy Harbor Island, where they were booked for two free outdoor concerts on a barge, the day before Super Bowl Sunday. Everything looked good.

Then the Gulf War broke out. All of a sudden, with the crisis in the Middle East, the Super Bowl didn't look like such a sure thing anymore. Everybody started talking about the security risks, terrorist threats; maybe Tampa Stadium would be a target. Maybe Saddam Hussein would drop a bomb on the troops that day or launch some Scud missiles at Israel. If that happened, nobody was going to want to watch football. So a few weeks before Super Bowl the word started to spread around Tampa like a cancer: "They might cancel the Super Bowl." The general feeling was: We can't have crowds down in sunny Florida watching football and drinking beer and having a fabulous time while everybody's sons and daughters and husbands and wives are out on the front line in some desert hellhole risking life and limb in 105-degree temperatures. It wouldn't look right.

But the city never stopped the beautification work. They never stopped planting those palm trees or preparing the city because of the millions of dollars that would be lost if the game were canceled. More security would have to be stationed at the stadium and at the airport. Suddenly, the whole city shifted to high-security alert. The game would go on.

The Tempts began arriving in Tampa on Wednesday. Dennis rolled up to the hotel in a white limo with his fiancée, Donna, who was a nurse and a nursing teacher. It didn't surprise me that Dennis had a fiancée even though he was not yet legally divorced from the last Mrs. Edwards. I have a saying that goes: "You are Very Motown if . . ." So when Dennis showed up I immediately thought, You are Very Motown if you have a fiancée and are not yet legally divorced. And Dennis *was* Very Motown.

Eddie was the next to arrive, alone as usual. David was due to arrive from Philadelphia that night, but with David you never knew. When I arrived at the hotel the next morning, which was the first day of rehearsals, I went directly to David's room, way down at the other end of the hall from everybody else's rooms. David gave me a big hug and a kiss. He was there with an associate of his from Philadelphia, whom he introduced as Butch, "my personal valet." I didn't know what was going on. Butch didn't look like a professional valet to me.

Butch started telling me his history: how he owned a limousine company in Philly, and he and David were best friends. He said he had limos at David's beck and call and that any time I was in Philadelphia he would put them at my disposal.

Then Butch told me, "You know, I've spoken to you before."

"When?" I didn't remember having had a conversation with this man.

"I'm Butch, Butch Murrell. Remember? Me and a friend of mine called you when David was supposed to do that show down in Miami at the Fountainebleau Hotel."

It all came flashing back to me. I just said, "Oh, that was you?"

We all left in two white Cadillacs for the stadium, and when we arrived, security guards had to search the trunk, look under the hood, frisk everybody, and check our armbands. When they finally let the drivers enter the parking lot, we only got stopped again so that stadium security people could check us all over again and have the dogs sniff everything they could get to.

We finally made our way into Tampa Stadium, through hordes of teenage dancers rehearsing, and production people brandishing clipboards and notebooks, and arrived at the dressing room, which was really a locker room. I had assumed that the Tampa Bay Buccaneers would have a sharp dressing room, perhaps with a barber shop, separate showers, catering facilities, and so on, because after all, they are superstar athletes. But this was just like an average high school locker room—not Very Motown.

I was told that for rehearsals all the entertainers would be sharing this one big, hideous team locker room—the former Temptations, Three Dog Night, and New Kids on the Block. Of course, the New Kids had an enormous staff and entourage. They seemed to be basically tightly controlled puppets, and without their baby-sitters telling them exactly what to do, they would have been lost. They reminded me of the Temptations and some of the other Motown acts in their early heydays; the grooming, the choreography, the isolation, the incredibly controlled situation, the brainwashing—but not the talent. They all seemed to have that huge, superstar attitude, as if their egos had preceeded them into the room, and they expected to be fussed over. Of course, they seemed to be genuinely taken by the ex-Tempts, because in so many ways that's exactly who they were modeled on.

As the day progressed we could all see that David was in increasingly bad shape. He looked and sounded like his asthma was killing him. Even with a baseball cap pulled down low over his head, his collar turned up high around his neck, and those large, trademark glasses of his, he looked horrible. People were coming up to me and asking, "What's the matter with David?" Or, "Does he have cancer? Does he have AIDS?"

I just kept reassuring them, "Oh, he just has an exceptionally bad case of asthma. He'll be fine." And I was certain he would be. Hadn't I seen David leap out of his hospital bed and onto a stage before? With all the TV cameras and the millions of people watching, with all the excitement that the guys were feeling because now, finally, they would have all this worldwide exposure and could really get a leap up on Otis—with all this going on, I was sure David could pull off another Baltimore.

Then the bomb dropped.

We were informed that the former Temptations would not be part of the half-time show, which would center around New Kids on the Block. The ex-Tempts were to be in the pregame show with the sixties group, Three Dog Night. Even worse, the pregame show was not going to be televised. There would be no millions of people watching.

We were also quickly discovering that the show had been scripted down to the last detail, so the guys would have no say at all in what they sang. From the moment they got there they were bossed around, told what to sing, where to stand, when to move. The producers had arranged and taped a very brief medley of songs. The guys had to lip sync the medley and adjust their dance routine to it. Nobody said much, but immediately I could feel the emotional letdown, as if the magic carpet had been pulled out from under their feet once again.

Being professionals, they did their rehearsals, and for the next two days they went back and did more of the same with new sets of armbands daily, the same intensive security checks, the same confusion going on around the stadium. Whenever they weren't rehearsing, David was locked in his room with Butch, and when they were rehearsing he continued to look very sick. I had to run out and buy him asthma medication several times.

Eddie stayed to himself in his room a lot of the time, not being bothered, while Dennis, Donna, and I took the limo and had a great time checking out restaurants, going to the mall, spending money, and talking. Dennis told me, "Don't pay Eddie no mind. He's acting weird. We don't know what's wrong with him."

I didn't know what David and Butch were doing in that room, because over these two days Butch handled everything at the door and would not let anyone in. I hoped that David was sleeping or resting, trying to get his strength together for the show.

The band and background singers were due to arrive at Tampa airport around 1 o'clock on Saturday, which was the afternoon of the outdoor concerts. According to Judas we didn't need to go to the airport; someone else was supposed to be meeting the group there. But since Dennis didn't need me and David was in seclusion, I decided to kill time and drive out to the airport anyway. Who should I see there but Judas! He looked shocked to see me.

Silently and separately we both waited for everyone to arrive, and after I had successfully taken care of the usual lost suitcase problems, Judas drove them off in a van with all their luggage. "Do you know how to get all the way out to their hotel?" I asked him.

"Yes, yes, you just go on back now. Maybe David could use you."

What seemed like hours later, and very late for sound check, they straggled in looking like road-weary refugees, still carrying their luggage.

"What happened to you guys?"

"This asshole has had us driving around downtown Tampa in the van for about two hours, looking for our hotel" Nate volunteered. "And he hasn't found it yet."

I said, "Your hotel is not in downtown Tampa!"

"That's what we kept telling him."

Everybody was tired and bitchy. Some of them had been traveling since six in the morning and had seen no lunch, no shower, no nothing. We did a quick sound check, and since by now it was way too late to get them back to the hotel to get ready, I arranged for them to be given the use of a room in the adjoining office building. A buffet was ordered, and just as everyone started eating and getting comfortable, in came Judas, announcing, "We're moving."

"Why are they moving?"

"Eddie said he don't want his people in some other people's office. He don't want nobody in his business."

"His business? What business? The office is empty."

Judas could offer no further explanation besides, "Well, Ed said. So all of you get out of this office. The singers and the band will be split between my room and Ed's room."

I knew Eddie was a person who didn't like to mingle, but this was ridiculous. We now had to pack up everybody's stuff and move next door to the hotel. Then everybody started taking quick showers while I went crazy trying to get them in and out of the bathroom because this was the eleventh hour and everybody in Tampa and their grandmothers would soon be there to see the former Temptations. In the middle of the chaos Dennis started panicking because he couldn't find his belt.

Ten minutes later a bewildered Judas came back. "Tony, I went down to David's room and he cussed me out through the door for no reason. Would you please take him this uniform for the show? He wouldn't let me in."

I went and knocked on David's door.

"What motherfucker is it?" he shouted.

"Godfather," I said, "it's me."

"Oh, it's you. Come on in." And he opened the door. "That Judas bitch came down here banging on my fuckin' door. Is he crazy? Nobody, not even you, bangs on my goddamn door like that!"

Very calmly, I said, "Here is your outfit."

"Hang it up there." He was just standing there in the doorway, motioning toward the closet and looking at me like a space cadet. So I hung up his outfit, and then raced back down the hallway to Dennis's room to look for his belt. Eddie, meanwhile, was going back and forth between his room and Dennis's, asking Donna repeatedly, "Can I bum a cigarette?" "Can I borrow a cigarette?" He had been doing this since Wednesday, and now she finally said to him, "Don't they sell cigarettes downstairs?"

"Yeah," he said, "but they cost two dollars and seventy-five cents." This was the same Eddie who had given a champagne birthday party for David Ruffin the previous year, and had asked all the guests for a five-dollar contribution.

"Well," Donna said, "don't you have a road manager? I'm pretty certain that he or Tony would leave the island and go across to one of the stores to get you some cigarettes."

"Never mind," said Eddie, storming out of the room.

Right on time, I rounded everybody up by the elevator to go down for the evening's first performance. I knocked on David's door. Butch answered. "It's Tony," I said through the door. "Is David ready?"

Butch opened the door a crack and stared at me. "David's not dressed," he said.

"Let me in."

David Ruffin had fallen asleep on a little child-sized cot over by the window. He was curled up in a fetal position and dressed in green surgical scrubs. Butch had obviously claimed the king-sized bed.

"Godfather," I told David, "you have to get up."

"Oh, God, I don't know what fuckin' time it is. Shit, it'll take me all fuckin' morning to get ready."

I've got trouble here, I said to myself. We had to be downstairs in exactly three minutes.

I gave Butch a look and told David again, "You have to get up. The promoter said that you will not be paid unless all three of you perform. Eddie will be upset."

"Fuck Eddie. Fuck the fuckin' promoter. I'm sick."

"David is so sick," Butch chimed in.

In my sternest voice, I said, "David, you have to get into your stage outfit." I turned to Butch, who was still standing there looking helpless. "Butch, where are his shoes? Where's his underwear? Lay everything out on the bed for him and get him into a cold shower, quick. I'll be back in a minute. In the meantime, spray some oil on his hair and try to get him together. You *are* supposed to be his valet, you know."

"Tony, I don't need no-motherfuckin'-body treating me like a fuckin' kid. You ain't my mother, bitch!" David screamed from his cot. "I can comb my own fuckin' hair."

I ignored him. "I'll be back in a few minutes or less," I said, bracing myself for Eddie.

Everybody else was still waiting in the hallway. "David's not ready," I told them. "There's a possibility that David's not coming." Eddie gave me a look. "What room's he in?" he asked me.

Eddie went down the hall and banged on David's door. I don't know what went on, but when he came back he announced, "David promised me he'll be down."

We went downstairs, were escorted through the tremendous crowd, got up on the gangplank that led to the barge which would be serving as the stage, and the show started. Right away, the promotion people started asking me, "Where's David? Where's David Ruffin?"

"Oh," I told them, "David doesn't come on until midway," and I went back upstairs, running through the audience, through the garage, and up into the hotel.

David was now sitting on the edge of the cot, stark naked and dripping wet. I asked him to put on his underwear and his jumpsuit. He rose, dried off, and put on his underwear. I helped him into the jumpsuit, hooked the belt around his tiny waist, finished styling his hair, dusted his face heavily with dark translucent powder, cleaned his glasses, and guided him toward the door. I didn't say a word, and neither did David. He gave me no resistance. He had completely changed in the ten minutes since I had left him.

As we went down in the elevator I could see David start to come alive. I noticed that he was picking up his tempo, and then he said, "Tony, run ahead of me and get my mike, because the second I get there I'm going right out on stage. Timing and style are all-important. Remember that New Year's Eve when I taught you that?"

"Definitely," I replied. "Style and timing, always crucial."

So I ran ahead, got the cordless mike, and turned it on. Close on my heels, David grabbed it from me and sailed out onto the stage in the middle of a number. The audience went berserk.

I saw a sign of relief pass across the face of the promoter, who thought that this whole thing had been staged. I saw relief in the band's faces, too. But I also noticed that David was not at his best during this performance. He made several small mistakes in the lyrics and dance steps, and he didn't look too well. I could see that he was hanging back out of the harsh glare of the spotlights. People were asking, "Why doesn't he move up?"

"He's got very bad eyes," I said, "and after all these years on stage the lights bother him."

David got through the first show. Before it came time to go back down for the second show I went to check on him. Boochie, the bass player, was standing in the hallway. "Where you going?"

I told him, "I'm going to get my godfather."

"Baby, your godfather's done gone."

"What do you mean, gone?" I thought he meant, left Tampa.

"Him and that creep that's with him. They went downstairs to the barge. He's good to go."

I said, "Oh God, I hope he's there."

Sure enough, we all went back down to the barge and there was David, in a fabulous mood. Two hours earlier he had been laid out in a fetal position; now he was the life of the party. He was joking around, kidding with everyone—"I fooled you all, didn't I?" he said. "I was late. But you motherfuckers are late this time! I should have fined your asses, but my name ain't Otis."

During the break between shows we had received a message that Frank Sinatra, who was doing a concert in town, wanted to meet "The Temptations." It was all set. A limo was waiting in the hotel's circular drive so that Eddie, David, and Dennis could do their second show, rush off the stage, change, and rush across town to catch the end of Sinatra's sell-out show. As soon as I heard about this my brain started clicking; I thought this opportunity was just too good to be true. Even if Frank Sinatra only wanted to shake their hands, at least it was a great photo opportunity. I asked Charles to get the car out of the garage in case any of the others wanted to go along.

The second show was over, and everybody was rushing like crazy to change out of their stage clothes and get downstairs to leave, when out of the blue Eddie, who was in one of his strange moods, decided, "Fuck Sinatra. I'm not rushing to see no Frank Sinatra."

I kept telling him, "This could be a great opportunity," and he kept looking at me like I was crazy. He just said "No, I've decided I'm not going," and eventually he got Dennis to agree with him.

"What's wrong with Eddie?" David wanted to know. By this time, he was dressed to the nines, on full alert, and all set to go. "Come on, David," I told him, "just you, me, and the background singers go." But now he was disgusted and he just said, "Fuck it, we all should be together. I don't understand why Eddie and Dennis don't want to go." I wondered what Eddie's reasoning could be. It certainly couldn't be the same excuse he had used when he, David, and Dennis were invited to join in a tribute to Billy Joel at the Grammy Awards ceremony. David and Dennis attended, but Eddie flatly refused, saying, "They're paying us fuckin' peanuts, and I'm not using my name to prop up another white boy."

So the whole meeting was blown, and we never got to meet the great Frank "The Voice" Sinatra, as his Hoboken fans used to call him. There was no way of knowing what was going on in Eddie's mind at times like this. It was another mystery. After all, what else did Eddie Kendrick have to do that night but hole up in his hotel room, take half the tobacco out of his cigarette, stuff it with cocaine, and smoke it? Eddie had always been able to keep his occasional drug use a well-closeted secret; he wasn't the type to let it get out of control, or to miss a show and risk not getting paid.

The next morning, Super Bowl Sunday, I went down to the hotel to meet the guys. The band had left Tampa early that morning, since they would not be needed for a lip-synched show. I took the escalator up to the lobby level, where I found Butch pacing the floor like a caged animal.

"Oh, hi, how are you doing?" I said.

"How do you fuckin' *stand* him?"

"Who?"

"Your so-called godfather! I own a limousine company, and I'm down here doing him a favor. I don't need his fuckin bullshit!" He was very irate.

I got him to sit down. "What happened?"

"That motherfucker threw me out! He threw me out last night and I had to sleep in the hallway, after all I did for him! That fuckin' bastard threw me out as good as I've been to him, he won't let me in to take a shower or change or nothin'. All the money I've given to him! I lent him my limos, I've saved his ass in Philly, I've been a good friend. He gets me out here on the road and he wants to pull some superstar shit with me? Fuck him!"

"Well, that's how David is, Butch," I said. "I'll go up and see how he's doing."

"Good luck," he said.

I went upstairs, knocked on the door, and David let me in. He seemed in a fine mood.

"What do you want to do with your Super Bowl ticket?" David asked me. We had all been given complimentary tickets to watch the Super Bowl after the pregame show. I told him, "I'm going to sell mine. There's a man downstairs who wants to buy two for twelve hundred bucks each."

"What! Sell mine, too!"

I went downstairs, sold the tickets, and gave David his twelve
hundred dollars.

When everyone was ready for the Super Bowl show we started
down in the elevator together and waited in the circular driveway.
As we were waiting, we saw Whitney Houston about to leave in her
limo, looking like a young girl out with her dad, and surrounded
by her female security guards all dressed up in what appeared to
be men's suits. She came toward Dennis and out of this cute, itty-
bitty thing came a voice like a steamroller. "You're the singingest
motherfucker I ever heard, baby!" she bellowed. "You could turn
out a fuckin' place!"

Dennis looked at me as if to say, Damn, isn't she kinda rough?
But he just said, "Thanks, Whitney. Are you staying for the game?"

"Hell, no! I've got my lover waiting for me back home, baby.
I'm getting a flight out of this motherfuckin' place right after I finish
singing the National Anthem." And she and her dad got into her
limo.

The show went according to plan, which was the most anyone
could hope for. The former lead singers of the Temptations came
dancing out from behind a giant jukebox, and they had to come out
at exactly the right second because the stage was moving simulta-
neously out onto center field. They did their short medley, and then
they had to exit at exactly the right second because if they didn't,
they were likely to be swallowed up by the stage that was now
splitting in half, or to be run over by the next act that was coming
on.

Later, back at the hotel, I was on my way up to David's room
when I saw Butch in the hallway. "That motherfucker threw me out
again," he said.

"Well, I don't know what to tell you, mister."

"Get me the fuck out of here! I'm leaving! I've had it with David!"

"Butch, I'm sure your flight doesn't leave till tomorrow morning."

"I don't care. I'm leaving now."

Butch left to go spend the night at Tampa International Airport. I planned to stay until the evening. As it started to get late David asked me, "Do you mind staying here at the hotel with me? Because I'm not feeling good, and I don't want to be alone."

I didn't mind. I figured it was just for one night. They were all supposed to leave early the next morning. David was booked on the same early flight as Butch, who I guessed was now trying to sleep on the airport floor.

Around six-thirty in the morning I started trying to wake David.

"Who the fuck told you to be wakin' me?"

"David, you gotta get ready to leave."

"Fuck it, fuck the guys, fuck the flight, fuck you. I'm not going. I'll take another flight."

I told him, "Your ticket is not good for another flight."

"Then you get me a new ticket. Shit!"

"Okay. All right, already."

"Now leave me alone. Why did you wake me up anyway, bitch? Are you crazy?"

I wanted to have breakfast with Dennis and Donna before they left. Eddie and Judas were leaving a little later. By noon everybody was gone—everyone except David Ruffin.

Super Bowl XXV was over. Before long the city would start returning to normal, the security would relax, all the extra help would be let go. The hotel was beginning to empty.

I went back to David's room. He was still asleep on the cot. Don't wake him, I told myself. I taped a note to the bathroom mirror, to the phone, and to the TV: 'At home. Tony Turner.' I hadn't come prepared to stay.

Chapter Twelve
Statue of a Fool

The game was over and the players had gone home. The TV crews, the reporters, the hordes of football fans, the cheerleaders, the performers—they had all packed up and left. But David Ruffin hadn't gone home. It was a pattern I knew too well. The only difference this time was that I was staying too, because I was already home.

That afternoon I had left David sleeping at the hotel and had gone home to wind down from five consecutive days of Super Bowl madness. Around five o'clock my private hot line rang.

"You have a lot of fuckin' nerve, Tony. You don't ever leave me anywhere with some note, bitch." David had woken up.

"Well, I'm sorry," I said. And quickly changing the subject, "You're going home, David. I've got you on a late-night flight tonight."

"I'm not going no-fuckin'-where. Didn't I tell you last month that

I wanted to find me a house here? You crazy or what?" And then he burst out laughing. "Oh, baby doll, you know I'm just fucking with you. Come on down! I feel like some barbeque—find us a barbeque place."

"You want to go out?" I asked him.

"Nah, nah, nah. Bring in some barbeque rib dinners."

My friend Charles drove me to the hotel, and we went directly upstairs. David was sitting statuelike on the edge of the bed hitting his crack pipe. Over on the desk was a big stack of money and a plastic bag of rocks. The room was a wreck, with clothes thrown around everywhere and empty food trays all over the place. Surprisingly, David had eaten everything in sight.

"Charles and I brought you your barbeque dinner."

"I don't want no fuckin' barbeque, bitch. I want a goddamn Big Mac with extra cheese and bacon."

Charles and I went back downstairs, left Harbor Island, found someplace open, and got David a cheeseburger.

Charles decided to wait downstairs in the car while I took the burger up to David.

"I don't want that! I done ate the barbeque ribs. You took too fuckin' long," he told me. "I ate my dinner and yours." I had never seen David eat like that. "I don't need you no more tonight," he said. "Go home and get yourself some rest. Here, take this money. It's your pay."

Thanking him, I told him I would call him in the morning.

"Bitch, don't you go calling me in the morning. Call me at two o'clock. As a matter of fact, have your ass here at one o'clock and have some real estate for me to look at. And don't be showing me nothing huge like that Diana Ross and the Supremes Rich and Famous shit, because that is too extravagant. I'm looking for a reasonably priced villa, something I can maintain by myself." He was being very realistic.

"Tony, I've got five good years left in me. I'm going to work hard, make money, buy me a home, and when that five years is up I'm going to retire while my voice is still good."

I asked him, "What about Diane?"

"Man, she's there. She's got her house fixed like a shrine to me—pictures of me all over. She wants me all to herself. I love her, but I can't live like that. I want to have a place of my own where I can come off the road and crash. I don't want to live with nobody, so no bitch can tell me to get the fuck out, or that I can't have certain people over at the house."

"Well, what about looking at a condo or a townhouse here on Harbor Island?" I asked him.

"I don't want no townhouse or condo. I want a villa with a private courtyard and a small swimming pool. Plus I want me a heated jacuzzi and two additional bedrooms so Nedra and the grandkids can come down. And I want a big, big living room where I can put a piano, maybe some drums, a big stereo unit and some recording equipment. Some place where my privacy and security can be assured. It's about time I had a home of my own again. Shit, I'm making good money these days."

David did make good money when he was able to work. It was just a question of the group getting enough jobs, and of David showing up. Since he was planning on getting himself straightened out and working hard, I saw no reason he shouldn't be able to buy the villa of his dreams. Besides, all you had to do was mention the name Temptations and allowances would be made. You didn't even have to go to the bank—the bank would come to you. You didn't have to beg for an easy-payment plan—it was placed in your lap. Who cared about credit histories!

Appointments were made, and the next day Charles drove David and me around looking at luxury villas. David was the perfect star. He could change like a chameleon, and today he was in his public appearance mode. At every sales center the people just loved him. He saw a villa that he fell for instantly in one of Tampa's most exclusive country club communities. It was an elegant courtyard home nestled beside the manicured emerald green of the golf course.

"I'll get me a golf cart," he declared as we toured the model, "and I'll join the country club." I thought, good God, they don't know who they're getting. "And call your Cadillac dealer friend in New York," he told me. "Tell him I want that Fleetwood Brougham I was going to order last summer, with the purple leather interior."

I didn't talk to David again until the following morning, which was the day he was now supposed to be leaving for Philadelphia. I telephoned to inform him that I was on my way over to his hotel to help him pack.

"I'm not going no-fuckin'-where. I'm too sick to travel. Come down right away."

I rushed to the hotel.

Opening the door, I found David in his now-familiar position on the bed, huddled over his pipe like an old man. The room was even more of a mess than it had been a couple of days earlier. He had piled breakfast trays, lunch trays, and dinner trays on the table until there was no more room there, then he had started piling them up on the floor. The hotel must have been running out of room service trays; they were all in David's room.

"You want me to call housekeeping?" I asked him.

He said he didn't want anyone coming into his room. But he didn't want to be alone. I wondered if that was why he kept the TV on the whole time.

I stayed with him and we talked. He wanted to know what I thought about the villa. I told him that I found it quite dramatic.

"Well," he said, "I'm also thinking of moving to Las Vegas. And if I do, you're going to have to sell that big fortress you live in, and move with me to Vegas."

David couldn't sit still. He would jump up in the middle of a conversation, pace around the room, and sit down again. He was all hyped up. He'd hit the pipe and talk about—who else?—Gordy.

"You know it was Berry Gordy who tipped off the IRS and got me busted and thrown in jail? He made me lose my fuckin' house in Detroit." There was no way of knowing the truth.

Every day was crazier than the last. I was constantly going in and out of the hotel on errands for David. The pile of rocks on the desk diminished steadily in size, the state of the room got progressively worse, and when I lay down to take a nap one time, I discovered that David was keeping a loaded nine-millimeter gun under the pillow.

The pipe was always in David's hands. He was still coughing, and although he was eating like a maniac, he looked thinner and more ill every day. The times when I called before I went down to see him and he wouldn't answer, I had to ask myself, is he dead, or did he leave town? When I checked with the hotel operator, she would tell me that Mr. Ruffin had not checked out. But David Ruffin was not a person who checked out. He would just suddenly leave. So I let myself into his room, never sure what I would find inside.

One day I let myself in and found a shattered mirror and a smashed flower vase lying among broken drinking glasses on the floor. The TV was blasting louder than ever, and David was playing around with the gun.

"Put that thing down," I said.

"You know Fred, Bill, and Isaac are watching me, bitch."

I asked David whom he meant.

"The FBI, stupid. And now they got the CIA on my black tail too."

"What do you mean, the CIA and the FBI are watching you?" I could hardly hear myself speak over the TV.

"You know, when I came through the lobby yesterday, those motherfuckers at the desk were giving me a curious look. Then I get in the elevator, and that manager starts bothering me, talking about the TV's too fuckin' loud. You curse that motherfucker out, Tony. He doesn't know who the fuck I am? Shit! As much money as they're charging a nigger like me to stay in this hotel! Shit! You might have to move me, baby."

I said, "Where's the remote control, David? We have to turn down the volume on the TV."

"I threw that thing out the window."

"Well, I'm gonna lower the volume."

"Bitch, you're just like somebody's wife. You ain't nothing but a nag."

As I went to lower the volume on the set, David said, "I broke the knob off."

"David, why did you break the knob off the TV?"

He jumped up with his crack pipe. "It's my motherfuckin' TV. Get your black ass in that bathroom. I want to show you something. You think I'm crazy? You'll see."

I went in the bathroom with David. "Get down on your knees like me." I got down on my knees in front of the vanity sink. "Look up under here. There's bugs in here."

I was thinking, cockroaches, but I couldn't see any.

"Don't you see that thing over there? That bug?"

"I don't see it," I told him.

"You low motherfucker. All the money I pay you, you blind bitch. Get yourself some good glasses. Forget them little contact lenses 'cause baby you can't see shit with them. Poor thing. God, baby doll!" Already his tone was changing. "Is it my fault, baby? You're blind as a bat. You can't see that FBI bug?"

Then it clicked in my brain what kind of bug he was talking about. I figured, why argue? Who am I not to agree? So I said, "Oh my God, I'm so crazy. Now I see it!"

"I told you! I can't find them all, but I destroyed about twenty of them. They're in the garbage."

We got up off our knees. "That's why I have the TV turned up so loud," David went on, "so they can't hear our conversations. That's why I had to break the knob off the TV. You know, the FBI, the CIA, and the IRS is looking for me."

"Poor Godfather," I said. "You're in so much trouble."

We sat down on the bed. "Here, you want a hit?" David asked me, offering me the pipe.

"No, thank you. You know I don't do drugs."

"Bitch. As much of my damn dope as you've stole from me over the years, and now you want to look down your nose at me because I'm taking something for my nerves." He started laughing, and I started getting scared. "You gotta be crazy! As much dope as you use. I know you used to do some coke, baby, because you done too much of mine. I ought to get my gun and blow your fuckin' brains out."

It's time for me to go, I told myself. I hated to see him like this, but I knew it was not in my capacity to help him escape it. I had started to think that perhaps David Ruffin, who had come so close to death so many times, was still not on his ninth life. Maybe he was somewhere on his fifth. He knew so much about drugs, about how to walk it off, how to bring down the high. He'd tell me, "Get me a brandy," "Walk me," "Get me coffee," "Run me a cool shower." But this time he didn't want to be separated from his pipe; he made no such requests.

"You need to stop," I told him. "You don't know what you're talking about. You know I don't use that stuff. Who wants to be bothered with all that pipe and water and confusion? That's too much work. I'd rather drink champagne, honey."

"I knew you did something, bitch. I just wasn't sure what it was." And then, "You sure you didn't take no dope from me?" I told him, no, and asked if he wanted me to get him anything.

"Go get me another one of them burgers. That one was so good."

"How was it good? When I got back you'd eaten the ribs and *I* ate the burger."

I went out into the night and got David another burger. As I walked back in through the lobby, the manager stopped me. "Mr. Turner, could I have a word with you?"

We went into his office. "May I speak frankly with you, Mr. Turner?" he said. "I see you coming back and forth all day. You are the only person that Mr. Ruffin lets into that room. He won't let the maid in, he won't let room service in. I've had reports from guests staying on that floor about all kinds of loud noises in the night. They say he's in there screaming, and we think he's having fits. We also believe there are several broken articles in the room. Now, we don't want to ask him to leave or call the police, but something must be done."

By the time I got back upstairs, David had calmed down some. I called housekeeping and asked them to send up a vacuum, a broom, something to pick up glass with, and fresh linen. While I cleaned up, David sat on the bed like a statue, seemingly unaware of anything.

I went to change the bed. "Stand up," I told him.

He stood up. "You're in a bitchy mood now," he said.

"That's right."

"I ain't gonna mess with you. You're worse than the FBI and Berry Gordy rolled into one."

I changed the bed, got all the debris out, and returned the equipment to the maid who was waiting right outside the door. "He's very sick," I told her. "He's on medication that makes him hallucinate."

He was restless. He kept hitting the pipe, then he'd eat some more, we'd talk. Half the time I was just beginning to understand what he was saying, when he'd suddenly change the subject. Half the time I was just sitting there listening to him because he wanted me there.

He told me the IRA was after him.

"You mean the IRS?"

"No, motherfucker, I mean the IRA." Some people from the Middle East were also looking for him. Berry Gordy, of course, was going to have him killed any second. "I'm telling you," he said, "before this year is out you're going to be in black."

"Well, I wear black a lot."

"What occasion, asshole? What occasion demands black, bitch?"

I had to think for a second. "A funeral? Oh, get out of here, Godfather. You need to stop that kind of talk."

He complained about how he was tired of getting robbed, how Berry Gordy had brainwashed and probably ripped them off all those years, how Gordy was rumored to have been hooked up with the Mafia, how he had ruined careers—Martha Reeves's, Mary Wells's, Brenda Holloway's, Flo Ballard's, and David's own—the same things I had been hearing for the past twenty years. But I listened, because if I didn't listen he would very sharply remind me that I was on a salary, and that my ass was being paid to sit there. "So shut the fuck up, and if I feel like talking about Berry Gordy for eight hours straight, you're going to listen."

He'd fly off the handle, then he'd calm down, and for a while he would be perfectly coherent. He talked about all the drug treatment programs he'd been to, and how he could teach them a thing or two about detox. He said it was just another way the white man had found of ripping off rich black people's money, nothing but a scam. "You can't cure no motherfucker like me in thirty days," he said. "I need to be locked up, but they don't know that."

He talked a lot about Tammi Terrell: how he had really loved her and how sorry he was about the way things had turned out.

"Because . . . because . . . because of the way I treated her, how she died, what could have been—that's why I'm so messed up, man." He believed she could have been the next Diana Ross, but Berry had ruined her career—he had put her on the back burner. David talked about how Motown was just using Tammi at that time to help propel Marvin Gaye's career, because Marvin was married to Berry's sister Anna, and Marvin needed some hits so Anna could have gobs of money.

Anyway, he continued, they couldn't have Tammi going solo; you couldn't have another girl getting big hits. What the hell would happen? Diana Ross would no longer be the top dog at Motown. But as long as Tammi was hooked up with Marvin Gaye it was fine. It was a duo, it was safe, and Diana could be top diva without any competition.

David said it wasn't true that he had hit Tammi in the head. People told that story, he said, trying to blame him for Tammi's death—people who didn't like him, who felt that Tammi was too good for him, that she was forsaking a solo career by running around in a mink-lined Cadillac with a crazy no-good drug addict like David. That was certainly not what Gordy had had in mind for her when he put Motown to work cleaning up her image.

"Gordy wanted to keep her away from me. He was tying to break my spirit because I refused to kiss his little short ass."

I started to understand how much David must have been hurt by false accusations. He was always seen as the bad boy, and everything was always his fault. Of course, David was no angel and I was sure he never had been, but like he said, "Someone from a little white group goes into treatment and they get put on 'The Tonight Show' with halos around their heads. I go into treatment and they take my bookings away from me." He was never patted on the back when he did things right. There was a double standard at work and David felt victimized.

He told me about how, ever since he was a kid, he had wanted to be a racing car driver. So he got really excited when the opportunity came for him and Eddie to enter a race that was being organized by the Just Say No campaign. They both did their training, and David was sure he was going to beat everyone because he was beating them in the trials, but when it came time to enter the race the organizers banned David because of his druggy reputation. David was in treatment at the time.

He told me that he had suffered since childhood from mental problems. I knew that David Ruffin had some problems having nothing to do with drugs. They were the problems of his past: the abuse he had suffered at Motown; abuse he had suffered while he was growing up; Tammi's death and the blame that had been put on his shoulders—those things that he so rarely talked about, but that dwelt deep inside of him. There was a part of David that you couldn't reach, yet there was also the part that reached out to you.

He spoke of events years and years before, then he would jump back into the present. He talked about the villa he was hoping to buy, and how he was going to straighten up. Then, suddenly, he said, "I'm going to sleep now. Don't leave and don't wake me."

David was still sleeping when I woke the next day. I called Dennis to tell him what was going on, and that the hotel manager wanted David out. "Don't get in it," Dennis told me. "Stay out of it. Go down to the manager's office and give him the management company's number. Let them take care of it."

I did what Dennis said, waited a couple of hours, and called him back. David was still out like a light. Dennis told me that the management company had been contacted. Somebody would be coming down to get David.

"How is he?" Dennis asked me.

"Bad, and there's plenty of drugs here."

"Get out of there," he warned. "Don't get mixed up in it."

Later, when David had finally gotten up and had something to eat, I told him, "I have to run up to my house and change my clothes."

"You don't have to go nowhere. I'll give you some money. Take this money and go to the mall and buy yourself whatever clothes you want."

"Well," I said, "thanks, but I've also got some business to take care of."

"All right. But call me in three or four hours."

Three or four hours later I called David from my home. A man answered. "I'm sorry, Mr. Ruffin is asleep now." I wondered how David had reacted to his arrival.

I called back around midnight and was met by the same answer: "I'm sorry, Mr. Ruffin is still sleeping. I'll tell him you called." When I tried again the next morning there was no reply. The front desk informed me that David Ruffin had left the hotel about five minutes earlier.

I hung up the phone.

David flew back to Philadelphia, where he disappeared into the bowels of the city for days, missing an engagement as usual. Eddie and Dennis went on and did the show without David.

This was the pattern of his life, a pattern I had long known but whose demons David had only just begun to let me understand. I will never forget the way he sat there on that bed for days, still as that statue made of stone that David wrote about in one of his early songs, a statue of a man who thought love had slipped through his hands, the statue of a fool.

Chapter Thirteen
Call Me

Long-distance call number one:

"Hi, Lamar, this is Tony. I'm sorry, I know Josie must have just gotten in the door from Europe, but I cannot wait to hear about what happened on this last tour." I always counted on the group's female background singer, Josie, for the unvarnished truth.

"I can't wait to see my baby either," Josie's husband, Lamar, told me. "I'm walking out the door now to pick her up from the airport."

"Well, I know she's gonna be totally exhausted, but would you please tell her that she's to call me the second she walks in the door, just so I can hear two little bits of facts about what went on?"

I knew that during Eddie, David, and Dennis's extended tour of Europe, David would once again be on trial, with Eddie as judge and jury. And I also understood from David that if he couldn't hack it this time, he would be out of the group again—Eddie had promised—meaning that I would be out, too. Without David Ruffin the former Temptations' pay would get cut substantially, and they wouldn't be able to afford to have me out on the road, no matter how bad they needed me.

Tired of pacing the house in my state of curiosity, I decided to take a swim. I must have been in my pool about two hours when the phone rang.

Long-distance call number two:

"Hi, Tony."

After a grueling tour and a long transatlantic flight, Josie sounded very tired. Her voice, usually crisp and vibrant, was raspy.

"Girrrl! How did it go?" I screamed.

"Baby," she said, "I'll give you one good idea. Some of the band members nicknamed the tour, 'The Magical Mystery Misery Tour.' Child, you ought to be glad you didn't go."

"Josie, don't you be saying that just to soften my feelings. Girl, you know I was dying to go."

David had planned for me to go on the tour, working for him and Dennis exclusively. But Eddie had had some major disagreements with Dennis and David about me. For some reason, Eddie suddenly hadn't wanted me out on that—or maybe any—tour. The only alibi offered to appease me came via Judas, who told me that things had got so messed up with the limited bookings that there just wasn't enough money to "drag" me out anyway. I recall raising at least one eyebrow at the word "drag."

"Honey," Josie told me, "We didn't know where we were going from day to day. Everything was totally messed up."

"Well, girl, I'll get all of that tomorrow after you've rested." Then I asked her, preparing for the worst—"How did my godfather David Ruffin do?" I hadn't seen David since Super Bowl and the aftermath in Tampa, although I talked on the phone to either him or Diane regularly to check on his spirits.

"Tony, we don't know and we can't figure out what happened to that man. Your godfather was terrific—I mean, absolutely beautiful."

"Girl, who are you talking about?" I thought that in her weary state she must have misunderstood me.

"David Ruffin!" she said. "Honey, he never missed a show, he never missed a beat. He was always right on time, and totally in control."

"You need to stop." I couldn't believe it.

"He just took over all the management business. He took care of our money and everything. In fact, he didn't come home with us."

"What? Did he stay in London visiting his brother Jimmy?" As we all knew, there wasn't anything unusual in David staying behind after a tour was over.

"No, child. He stayed behind because the promoter tried to give us a check for the final payment at the end of the tour, and David said he was not taking no check. He wanted cash, honey. He was staying in England until the next day, when he and the promoter were going to the bank to cash that check."

"Eddie and Dennis left David alone to get the money?"

"Judas is with him. Anyway, baby. I'm not really worried, because David's been quite professional."

"Amazing," I said. "Well, let me let you go get some rest. I'll call you tomorrow, or you call me." And I hung up thinking, quite interesting, quite interesting. Perhaps a little too interesting.

My conversation with Josie prompted me to immediately make long-distance call number three, to a member of the band.

"Hi. This is Tony. How did it go? Don't spare me!"

"Oh man, it was fucked up," he told me. "Totally fucked up. Some of the jobs fell through after we got there. For some unknown reason, Eddie was a total bitch, just acting stupid. Not like his old self at all."

"Really? How was David?"

"Tony," he said, "I kept David off all drugs. I held his money for him. David told me, 'Keep my money for me, because I don't want to buy any more of that shit.' I kept all those European drug dealers far away from him. After the shows, David would sit up with us until all hours. He was drinking a little brandy here and there and playing cards all night. He never kept us waiting like he usually does. There was no more sitting on a hot bus for hours waiting. Tony, David was in top-notch form." This was the second glowing report, and I felt it would just get better.

"David didn't look all that great some of the time," he went on, "but he was really trying hard. He was basically running the whole damn show. Now, I still don't know if I would have left David over there to get the money," he added, which was just what I'd been thinking. "But he's supposed to be coming home today. Judas is supposed to get Ed's and Dennis's cuts of the money from David and send them on. That's really why he was left behind. Now, I don't know if David's new attitude is going to continue once he gets back to Philadelphia"—the same thoughts had crossed my mind—"but he was great, and he was singing his ass off. David wants to update the show. He tells me he's getting himself totally clean. He's ready to work hard again. He wants to amass some good money. He says he wants to buy himself a brand-new house down in Florida."

I remembered Super Bowl, and the villa that David had fallen in love with.

"He told me that you're going to be taking care of him on and off the road."

"David said that?"

"Yeah, he's going to bring you out on the road right away. We're going back to Europe in June. But don't say I told you. You know he'll want to tell you himself."

I had to ask, "What was wrong with Eddie?"

"He was just acting like an asshole."

I knew the answer before I heard it. Ever since Super Bowl, and even before, I'd been hearing stories about how bitchy Eddie had become, how he'd fly off the handle at the slightest and oddest things. I wondered what had happened to the cool, easy-going Eddie Kendrick I once knew—or thought I knew. In fact, nobody could claim to really know him.

"And how was Dennis, the Big D?"

"Dennis was Dennis. He was just in the middle, trying to keep a balance. But the main thing was that David was performing. It was the best I've seen him work an audience in years. He was the number-one Temptation, a true example of a total entertainer."

We spoke a while longer, covering this and that, and then Dennis Edwards called me.

Long-distance call number four:

"Hello, Tony?"

"Dennis, how was the tour?"

"Don't ask. It was sort of disorganized."

"How was Eddie?"

"Well, you know, Eddie was Eddie." Dennis sounded up, but apprehensive.

In my best haven't-heard-a-thing voice, I asked, "And how was David?"

"Man, David was great! I still can't hardly believe it. David didn't fuck up one time. You do know he took over everything from Eddie's boy?"

"No!" I said, trying to sound shocked. "Really?"

"Baby, it's true. I got great news for you. You're definitely going on the next tour, so don't worry about that."

Over the next few days, I wondered whether David had made it back to Philly and if he had come back with Eddie's and Dennis's shares of the money—because Dennis, too, had mentioned that he was a little nervous about the whole arrangement. He knew that David had arrived back in the States, but since then he hadn't heard a word.

Long-distance call number five: perfect timing—David had just arrived home. His voice sounded crystal clear. As we talked about the tour and its ups and downs, David proudly volunteered the information to me about staying behind for the money. He seemed up and positive. He told me that he had spoken with Eddie and Dennis about me coming back on the road, and assured me it was all settled.

I spoke with David several more times over the next few days about arrangements for me to go back out on the road with them. He sounded completely coherent and on his job. He was very excited about the upcoming European tour. We would be traveling all over Europe, including Yugoslavia, Italy, Vienna, and Amsterdam. "It's going to be great!" he said.

So I called the booking agent in New York and asked her to send my tickets. That, I believe, was long-distance call number eight.

Long-distance call number nine: David sounded to me like he was in a phone booth in a club or something, because there was a lot of noise in the background. "Did you hear anything from Ed or Dennis?" he asked.

I told him, no. Not a word. Suddenly, I sensed that something was strange with David.

"I know they're talking about me. I know they're saying that I'm not going to send them their money. I got their damn money, I just been busy. I didn't touch their fuckin' money. I didn't even touch my money." He no longer sounded perfectly coherent to me, and I became slightly alarmed.

He said, "I'm sending them their money tomorrow, by Western Union. I bought me some bad new outfits. And I bought sneakers, some Bermuda shorts, and silk summer shirts to go on the next tour." David's outfits, unlike Eddie's or Dennis's, could sometimes be a little questionable.

"I bought me a beautiful gold cross too," David went on. "I paid a fortune for it, but it came on this thin little gold chain. Well, you can't wear no heavy cross like this on a thin chain. So anyway, I put the cross in my shirt pocket, but tomorrow I'm gonna get me a real chain."

I said, "David, don't you be getting one of those L.L. Cool J–style gold chains."

"No," he told me, laughing. "I'm gonna get me a Mike Tyson–style chain. Tony, you're gonna love this cross. It's twenty-four carat gold, and it's got brilliant, blue-white diamonds all over it."

David loved flashy, expensive jewelry. He'd once had a gold Rolex watch with a face all covered in diamonds. He loved beautiful, large diamond rings, especially pinky rings, that he always kept in this slimline briefcase together with the other pieces of his transient life—his paper work, his current contracts, tons of assorted airline tickets for missed flights, passport, asthma medication, money, cologne, comb, and a Bible. I remember times he would open up that briefcase, and you'd see a shirt and tie come up out of it. It was unbelievable what you could find in its small confines. The thing weighed a ton. I used to think it must be lined with lead.

So I told David, "You should take that cross out of your shirt pocket and put it in your briefcase before you lose it."

"How you know I got my briefcase with me?"

"Godfather, your briefcase to you is like a pocketbook is to a woman, and I know you never go anywhere without that heavy thing."

"You're right, God is with me," he said. "I'm going to do that. I'm going to put my cross in my briefcase." And he went on to talk about religious and spiritual matters, closing the conversation with, "Tony, some of the things we are both looking for are the very things we don't need. Always depend on God. And call me."

I felt relieved.

On Friday night I went out and was driving home late, when I had a sudden urge to make long-distance call number ten to David from the car. Dialing Diane's number, I happened to look at the clock on my dashboard. It said 3:55 A.M.; for some reason, that number stuck in my mind. So I decided, no. I aborted the call, drove on home, and went to bed.

Long-distance call number eleven: Half asleep, I reached for the phone and peeked at the clock. Nine o'clock, Saturday.

"God, I don't know, Tony, I don't know."

It was Dennis, and for Dennis to call at 9 A.M. meant he had waited to call, because Dennis was in the habit of getting up at 6 A.M. and going jogging, getting his paper and breakfast, and calling me.

I said, "Don't know what?"

"I don't know, baby doll. This might be some bad news. Your godfather's fucking up."

I struggled my way up out of the multitude of pillows on my king-size bed. "What happened?"

"Well, you know David stayed over there in Europe and came back with that money," Dennis said. "I spoke with Judas this morning, and he did not get my money or Eddie's money from David. He said that David wouldn't give it to him. David kept everybody's money and promised he was gonna send it through Western Union. But me and Ed have been calling down there to Diane's house like crazy, and Diane says she ain't seen David in days. We haven't been able to catch up with Ruffin."

"Lord," I said, "I hope he ain't out with those vagabonds he hangs out with. You know, if David has time and money on his hands, that could spell double trouble."

"That's what we're thinking. David done got with some of his crew of bloodsuckers. Ed is pissed about the money," he went on. "That's me and Eddie's last piece of money. You know, we didn't make as much as we were supposed to over there because some gigs got canceled, so Tony, we *need* that money. If that damn David don't come up with it, I think Ed is going to be through with him and could put him out of the group permanently. And if he's out of the group, that means our next European trip could be in jeopardy. Or they might want to pay us less. And you know what that's going to mean—"

I sat straight up in bed with my back against the cold mirrored wall. I knew what that meant. That meant I could be out, too.

Well, I had been on and off the road so many times by this point that whenever they told me they would take me on tour, I didn't even acknowledge it as a fact until I had actually gone, got paid, and returned home. Besides, I had a life of my own and certainly didn't live through the group.

I told Dennis, "No, he'll come through with the money. You know what he'll do. If he spent the money, all he'll do is get together with Eddie, and he'll say, 'You can take the money I owe you out of my earnings on the next tour' ".

"I don't know if Ed's gonna go for it," Dennis said. "Because you know how David runs that game all the time. He tells you that, and then when he's out on tour he starts a big fight and wants all his damn money. That's a crazy motherfucker. I don't know what we gonna do with him."

We started to jive talk about David, going over some of his more crazy antics that had kept us all amused, amazed, and aghast.

"Lord have mercy," I sighed.

Dennis took a deep breath. "Call me."

So there I was, laying across the bed, half awake and mostly asleep, swearing aloud to myself. I knew that shit had been too good to be true about me going back on the road and about David's new attitude.

I realized that somehow I had to be wide awake, so I threw open the patio doors and jumped, buck naked, into the pool. Refreshed from my swim, I resolved to get to the bottom of this mystery.

Long-distance call number twelve: Diane's line was busy. I hung up, planning to try again in a moment. By now I was feeling anxious, and needed to talk with somebody. So I called my mother. I told her what Dennis had said and how although I had recently talked to David, nobody could find him now. Suddenly I remembered his recent call about the gold cross. I was just relaying this conversation to my mother when my call waiting signal beeped.

Long-distance call number fourteen. "Tony, did you hear?"

"Hear what?"

"Child, sit down. I got something to tell you."

So I went back to my mother and told her, "I'll call you later. Josie's got something to tell me." I had no idea what this bit of news that I had to sit down for could be.

"Tony," Josie went on, "Lamar just called me."

"Yeah," I said.

"He just heard on the radio that *David Ruffin is dead!*"

"What? David Ruffin's not dead! I was just speaking to Dennis about David fifteen or twenty minutes ago—" The phone beeped. "Hold on, girl," I told Josie.

Long-distance call number fifteen: it was Dennis again.

"Tony, did you hear?" People always think I hear things automatically. I started to relay what Josie had been telling me on my other line, but before I could finish he blurted out, "David is dead. David is dead, Tony."

"What? Did somebody shoot him? Oh, no!"

"No, David was taken to the hospital. I don't know, it's very sketchy. They say he took an overdose."

"Wait a minute. Are they sure they got David Ruffin?" I couldn't believe it. "David Ruffin ain't took no overdose! Hold on a minute," and I got back to Josie on the other line. "It's Dennis, Josie," I told her. "He says David is dead from an overdose."

Suddenly we both just started screaming and crying together through the phone lines. "You better get off the line—I better go back to Dennis."

"Call me, Tony," said Josie.

"Dennis, are you sure?" I was near hysteria. I just couldn't take it in. Dennis told me, "Yeah. They said a stretch limo dropped him off at the hospital and took off." Right away I pictured a body being thrown out of a speeding limo. Later I would find out that the driver had stopped in front of the hospital emergency room door just long enough to give someone David's body and let them lift him, unconscious, out of the limo before it sped off.

"Nobody knows who was driving the limo," Dennis went on, "and they say David didn't have any ID on him. The police had to confirm his identify by checking his fingerprints with the FBI after they'd sent his body to the city morgue with a John Doe tag on his big toe."

"Oh my God! Oh my God!"

I was trying to calm down a little now. At the same time, a mystery was unfolding, and my mind was already jumping into action. I told Dennis about the call from David when he'd told me about his gold cross, and how he had everybody's money and was sending it out on Friday.

"Well," Dennis said, "they say he ain't had but fifty-three cents on him." Later that report would change to fifty-three dollars.

"Where's his briefcase?" I wanted to know.

"They didn't find no briefcase."

"Then something's wrong, because you know that David Ruffin don't go nowhere without that briefcase."

"Well, everything is up in the air right now. They're talking about doing an autopsy. Tony, I don't believe David overdosed himself. There's some foul play here. I gotta call Ed. I'll call you later."

I hung up the phone and was getting ready to call my mother back, when I received long-distance call number sixteen.

It was some tabloid magazine. "Tony Turner, please. I was told that I could call a Mr. Turner about the Ruffin overdose."

"I'm sorry, you got the wrong number." These reporters are fuckin' vultures, I thought.

Wait a minute, wait a minute. There's something wrong. Let's look at the facts. David Eli Ruffin is dead. Tens of thousands of dollars are missing. He was thrown out of a stretch limo, the limo disappeared, they don't know who the driver was. Was he dead when the limo got him to the hospital? The briefcase is missing. He must have had the money in the briefcase. Was he robbed? Did somebody rob and overdose him?

There is Big Trouble here, I told myself.

Long-distance call number seventeen: I called a friend of mine who works in a lawyer's office. We were busy developing theories when my phone beeped. Putting my friend on hold, I took long-distance call number eighteen.

"Tony!"

It was Scherrie, who used to date Dennis Edwards. The news bulletin had just interrupted her daughter's Saturday morning children's show.

"What did they say?" I asked her.

"That David Ruffin was found dead in a crack house."

"A crack house? He was not in no crack house! Dennis just told me he died at the University of Pennsylvania Hospital."

"No, they said he was in a crack house, and he was taken unconscious from the crack house in a limo. Who would take a limo to a crack house?"

"Well, that's David Ruffin," I said. "David always liked to be driven in a stretch limo. After he sold Diane's Lincoln Continental town car to that kid for twenty dollars, I know she ain't hardly gonna let him use her car."

"But you know what, Scherrie," I went on, "That Butch man, he told me he owned a limo company."

I went back to my friend on the other line. "Remember I told you about that man who claimed he was David Ruffin's manager back in December, and came down to the Super Bowl. Well—"

Everybody started trying to figure it out. We all had theories.

Nobody could believe that a veteran drug user like David, even with his respiratory problems, could accidentally overdose himself. We all thought it had to be murder.

Long-distance call nineteen: Diane sounded stunned, almost to the point of calmness. She was shocked but, like many of us, not surprised. Diane had heard the news from the booking agent, Ruth Bowen, who was also in shock because she had been in touch with David just a few hours before he died, and everything seemed fine.

Diane told me that at first she didn't believe Ruth. She thought this was one of David's pranks. She found out it was true when she called the mortuary, to confirm the news. She'd wanted to rush right down there, but there were already too many reporters crowding outside her house. Her phone had not stopped ringing since. "I've even been cussed out. I don't know what is going on."

Beep: another call on her line. We hung up, knowing we would call each other many times over the next several days.

Call twenty: Dennis. He still couldn't believe that David overdosed himself. "He knew more about drugs than any doctor."

"Have they found his briefcase?" I asked.

"I don't know."

"I wonder if he had the money in it?"

"No. David bought a money belt so the money wouldn't get stolen. Supposedly, he put the money in the belt. But the hospital officials say they didn't see any money belt. Tony, I bet somebody killed David for that money. I'm telling you now. Somebody probably purposefully overdosed him to get at that money."

"How's Ed holding up?" I asked Dennis.

"Ed is extremely upset. I don't care about the damn money, but we all want this thing investigated. You know, with David's reputation they're going to try to blame it on drugs and sweep it under the rug quick just like they did with the Paul Williams death."

By now it was afternoon and the phone had not stopped ringing. Long-distance calls twenty-one to thirty-six were just miscellaneous hysteria calls—fans and friends offering condolences, and people that try to exploit any situation, including the tabloid reporter who called me two more times, and a top gossip columnist.

Just then I realized that I had not yet spoken to David's daughter, Nedra. I was just getting ready to pick up the phone and call her home in Detroit when long-distance call number thirty-seven came in from my business manager, Pat.

"What in the world is going on, Tony?" she said. "Detroit is at a standstill. Everybody is horrified over this David Ruffin story. Listen, Tony," she told me, "everybody is saying that David didn't overdose himself—that David Ruffin knew drugs. People here are saying that this story has to be checked out, that it more likely could have been murder."

I told her how Dennis had called me early in the morning and how we had been joking about David and his exploits, unaware that at the very same moment the man was dead.

"Yeah, they say he died about 3:55 A.M."

"Good Lord," I said, "That's when I looked at the clock on my dashboard. Listen, Pat, I gotta call Nedra. Call me."

Long-distance call number thirty-eight: Nedra's line was busy so I just kept redialing and redialing and redialing until I finally got through to her and the two of us started screaming and crying almost in unison.

"Tony, my daddy didn't take no overdose," she insisted. "My daddy did not accidentally kill himself. They are wrong and something has to be done. They are wrong."

"I'm with you," I said.

"I have to start making arrangements, Tony. What am I going to do?"

"Well," I told her, "it's probably going to fall to you to plan everything. But whatever help you need, just call me."

"You need to get up here right away," she said. "People have been coming to the house nonstop, reporters are all over the place,

TV cameras are everywhere. They all want exclusive interviews—they want us to speak right away. How did these people find out where we live?" She sounded very panicky.

"We don't dare go outside," Nedra continued. "I can't let my children outside. We're all very upset. I don't know what's going on. They're banging on the doors, they're peeking in the windows—"

All the time I was talking to Nedra on the phone I could hear it beeping, beeping, beeping with calls coming in. But she was not taking those calls.

"The place is packed," she said. "We can't let any more people in here, there's no room to put them. And our friends that we want to come in the house can't get through the media crowd."

I was astounded. None of us would ever have expected people to go crazy like this over David Ruffin, and none of us was really prepared for the days ahead.

"Don't say too much to the press," I warned Nedra. "Because we don't know the full story yet. The medical examiner will want an autopsy done, I'm sure."

"It's crazy," she said. "Tony, I got to get these other calls. But don't forget to call me."

Over the following days the calls were frequent and intense—countless calls between myself and Diane, Dennis, Nedra, and Margarette. It seemed like we were all on the phone twenty-four hours a day. Wherever I was in my house—on the patio, in the bedroom, in the office, even in the garage—any place I was, I had that cordless phone with me. But I never called Eddie. I couldn't imagine how he might be taking it, and I decided to wait until we were face to face.

Margarette, who was very emotionally overwrought, told me during one of our phone conversations that David had called her on Friday evening just before his death, telling her he was doing fine, and that everyone would be getting their money by bank time on Monday. He also told her about his new cross. They stayed on the phone for about three hours, with David reading passages to her from the Book of Revelations.

"I believe David died of neglect," Margarette said during one of our conversations. In her opinion as a drug counselor, David risked dying every time he hit the pipe. In his condition especially, he was dancing with death most of his life. But information had emerged suggesting that David's death had something to do with his asthma. He might have fallen sick in the crack house, lay down, and when someone went to check on him he was unconscious.

Margarette knew only too well that David wasn't too proud to beg when he felt sick. He had always demanded what he needed, and if he needed to get to a hospital, he made sure he was taken. In her view, David died because nobody helped him. It was a terrifying thought. All those years people wanted to hear that Ruffin voice, a voice that had always resounded with some kind of lingering inner pain, and he ended up dying because no one would listen.

During another conversation I learned that David had called his old girlfriend Debbie from London and told her that he would be back soon, and wanted to go out to the farm after he took care of some business in Philadelphia. David always knew he could go back to the farm if he needed to, and Debbie knew that when David asked to come back, it was because he was in trouble and needed help.

Diane was in Philadelphia, taking care of things by phone with Martha Reeves's help and support. She was besieged, just like Nedra was besieged in Detroit. Fans were flying in from England and going directly to her home. The media had practically set up camp there. Philadelphia was pressing for a memorial service and a public viewing of David's body, because David was well known there. Crowds were gathering outside the funeral home where David's body was being embalmed. Feelings were so strong there that the mayor had to arrange for police security to keep the fans out.

The airwaves were full of David. People were screaming and crying, speculating and gossiping. People who had not given a damn about David for years began giving interviews and talking about him in what seemed to be a weird state of excitement, some singing the praises of the man they really loved to dog, while others lamented the passing of a man who, it seemed, had simply lived life too fast.

The media covered the Ruffin death fully, interviewing Philadelphia singer Gene McFadden as he stood amid a crowd of people watching police search the three-story, "celebrity" crack house where David had collapsed. Neighborhood people described how clients of this crack house had the nicest cars and even limos; how the place, which from the outside looked very run-down, on the inside had large-screen TVs, exercise bikes, expensive stereo equipment, and all the luxuries a big spender would expect. Nevertheless, no drugs or money were found in the house.

By Sunday the police had questioned Butch and cleared him of any suspicion. According to Butch, David had stashed the money in his office for a few days after he returned from London, and then retrieved it. On the Friday before he died, David had shown up at the office with another man who had been driving him around for several days, and borrowed a white stretch limo for the night. The driver was found, questioned, and cleared of suspicion. Though the disappearance and whereabouts of the forty thousand dollars remained a mystery, the police seemed to be very quickly coming to the decision that David had simply overdosed.

Dennis called me, saying, "Tony, Eddie's heard that David's briefcase was found in the crack house, and he called Butch and told him to get it and take it to Diane's." Neither the money nor the money belt had reappeared.

Diane got a call from Nedra, who wanted her to look in her

father's briefcase and find the diamond earring he wore on stage, which he kept in a double-barreled contact-lens case. Diane found the lens case. In one side was the diamond earring. In the other, a stash of cocaine. Also in the briefcase, apparently, was a note written by David, basically saying: I'm scared, somebody is out to get me, if anything happens to me look into it. When someone from the Ruffin family asked the police to enter the note into the file, the police apparently told them there was no point because the case was now closed.

Nedra was making arrangements for David's funeral in Detroit, and I had become her sounding board.

"Tony, what do you think about this? I think I'm going to bury Daddy with his glasses on."

"Well, Nedra, to tell you the truth, I never really saw him without his glasses on, except when he was asleep. He wouldn't look right to people without his glasses. They were like his trademark." So that was decided.

Another call: "Tony, what clothes should I bury Daddy in?" David had been wearing a lime green shirt, sneakers, and shorts when he collapsed.

"Well, it should be a tuxedo, you know. He has to go in a tux. Something formal." It was decided that David would be dressed in a new tuxedo.

"Tony, I need your help." It was Nedra again.

"What happened?" I asked her.

"We can't raise enough money for Daddy's funeral. We're going to have to hold a press conference tonight and let the public know that we need money to bury him."

"Nedra, honey," I almost screamed, "it cannot be done. You simply cannot let it out." I triggered back to that old Motown thing, 'You must never tell. Keep it in the family.' "It's just too embarrassing to your father's memory," I told her. "We have to find some other way. What about Eddie and Dennis? What about Melvin and Otis? Surely they might help in some way."

"Don't nobody have any money, Tony."

"Did you ask Berry Gordy? He's got money, and I can bet he would send some right away. If nothing else, it would be bad for his public image to have David buried without a decent funeral."

She hadn't asked him. I told her, "Nedra, let's make a list of possibilities, and put Gordy at the top. You've been doing well so far, girl. You've been holding yourself together—"

"I want to see him. I just want to see him. The autopsy's over, and he's still on ice in Philadelphia—we're getting desperate!"

"Honey, you have to be strong, you've got business to take care of. Somebody has to come through; we cannot go out there with a tin cup. That's all the media wants now. Call Martha Reeves," I told her. "She knows people at the Rhythm and Blues Foundation, and I heard they gave Mary Wells something like $125,000 to help her with her medical bills and get her set up in an apartment. Try any Motown insiders. Try the Four Tops, maybe Stevie Wonder. What about Aretha Franklin? Call her church. If some of these people give, you can have a nice, elegant, dignified funeral. Call them and see what happens, but don't hold any press conferences until we speak again. Call me!"

Thankfully, hours later I had another call from Nedra. "Baby, our worries are over." She sounded relieved, almost relaxed.

A casket company in Atlanta, the same company that had made the Reverend Martin Luther King's casket, had offered to donate a very expensive one for David.

"Well, honey," I said, "Thank God it's something decent, because we can't have David laid out in any old thing. It wouldn't be right."

"Baby," she replied, "they told me it's gonna be custom-made. I'm thinking of having it done on the outside in black patent leather."

"Mm," I said. "Wait a minute, honey. Ain't that a little . . . different?" I knew David was a fool for patent leather shoes. He must have had hundreds of pairs in his lifetime. "Can they *make* a patent leather casket?"

"Oh yeah, honey. The man said they could cover it right over the steel in black."

"Don't you think that might look very gauche?"

"I don't know," she said. "I might have a big pair of eyeglasses hooked up on top of the casket. Don't you think that's a good idea? Ain't nobody ever seen a casket like that."

"No, they haven't," I told her. "I don't know if you would need the glasses, though."

"What about if I just put his name on it?"

"That's a must."

"Well anyway, I got better news than that. Baby, Michael Jackson's paying for the whole funeral!"

She explained that her sister, Lynnette, had been put on phone duty, and one of the first performers she had called was Bobby Taylor, the singer who had supposedly been the one who had really discovered the Jackson Five and brought them to Motown.

"All I can give you is five hundred dollars," Bobby told Lynnette. "But call Michael Jackson and tell him your situation. I'll bet he'll be able to kick in some money. I know Michael always loved David Ruffin. He looked up to him like an idol when he was a kid. He used to copy some of David's early dance steps."

According to Nedra, when Lynnette called Michael Jackson's office the person on the receiving end was very nasty and very irate—"Who gave you this number? Who gave you this number? Who told you to call me?" Lynnette very nervously explained the situation and asked that the message be given to Michael Jackson. "Okay, I'll pass on the message," the person barked, and slammed down the phone.

So, Nedra told me, they scratched Michael Jackson off the list.

Shortly thereafter the phone rang. It was Michael Jackson. He told her not to worry about a thing, and not to take a penny from anybody because he was taking care of all costs, and he wanted everything to be top-notch. He did not want to see David Ruffin be put away in just any kind of fashion. He was very upset about David's death. He also said that, regretfully, he would not be able to attend the funeral himself because he felt that his presence would turn it into even more of a total media circus.

Everything seemed to be falling into place.

Dennis called. He wanted me to change the band's travel arrangements so that they could all get from their engagement in Virginia to the funeral in Detroit, and then back home. "Also, book us a hotel for one night. Then call me."

I had just started to make the airline reservations when Dennis called again: "Don't do it, Tony. Eddie wants his boy to handle it. And cancel any hotel arrangements you already made. Eddie wants us all to stay in Livonia at the Embassy Suites. He doesn't want to stay in Detroit. He wants to stay away from the reporters, and to avoid being interviewed if at all possible. If you hear anything else, call me."

Finally, on Wednesday, June 5, four days after his death, David's body was ready to be shipped to the Swanson Funeral Home in Detroit where his custom-made casket now awaited him. Diane was to accompany his body with all of his belongings, traveling by plane from Philadelphia. David's son, David Ruffin, Jr., and his brother, Jimmy, were waiting in Detroit.

David had returned to the Motor City that had once been and always would be home, to the forgotten city that would never forget. Detroit still claimed David Ruffin as its own. But David's adoptive family, Motown, had gone in search of warmer, whiter, wealthier pastures, and had long ago abandoned to doom both the city and the adopted son.

I packed my bags and prepared to leave for Detroit.

Chapter Fourteen
You Are Still in It

It was evening as David Eli Ruffin, laying in his traveling casket, arrived in Detroit, was met by the undertakers, and began to make his way under escort to the Swanson Funeral Home on Detroit's West McNichols Road. Following behind the hearse was Diane, accompanied by Martha Reeves. Diane was carrying David's patent leather show shoes, which were to be placed on his feet for the funeral.

As soon as it was reported that David Ruffin's body would go on public view on Thursday, the line of fans began to form outside Swanson's. He had died on Saturday, June 1, 1991. He was finally coming home to Detroit on Wednesday, June 5. By now there had been five full days of nonstop media hype, and continued rumors of his murder were fanning the gossip on the street. The whole situation was growing steadily out of control.

The private family viewing was set for Friday. I finally decided to leave on the first flight Saturday morning. I had changed my flight plans so many times already. I just didn't want to go, I didn't want to be faced with the reality of it. But finally, after a nerve-rattling, aborted takeoff, we got under way, and I arrived in Detroit and was met at the airport by Pat, who took me directly to the funeral home.

I could not believe the crowd that I saw as we approached Swanson's. I'd heard that the viewing line was very long, but I never expected anything like it and evidently neither did Swanson's. Diane had told me that when she had gone there on Wednesday with Martha Reeves and had told one of the funeral home ladies who she was, the lady had spoken to her very nasty and mean, at which Martha had snatched off her sunglasses and said, "I am Martha Reeves!"

"Oh, I'm sorry, Miss Reeves. I didn't know it was you."

"I don't care who you thought it was," said Martha. "Get Mr. Swanson up here right now. You're not supposed to speak to anybody like that. This young lady here is David Ruffin's fiancée. This woman has waited on David Ruffin hand and foot since Detroit arrested him and threw him out, and you should never talk to anybody or treat any of David Ruffin's fans like that. We Motown people have manners and always treat people well. You really should be ashamed of yourself standing in a funeral home and speaking to human beings in that manner!"

The driver pulled up at the side of the funeral home. The place was swamped. There were people of all ethnic backgrounds and all ages waiting in line, from babies in strollers to grandmas using walkers. Everybody was extremely orderly, very solemn, and I suddenly got nervous; I knew that what I was about to see would be totally upsetting.

Pat, who had called in advance to make arrangements for my visit, took me straight into the cavernous viewing room. I could see David's body quite plainly as I entered the room, although I was about fifty feet away from him. He was lying in state in a little roped-off alcove at the very end of the room, in a magnificent, solid steel casket, open from head to toe. He looked like he was lying on an expensive quilted sofa.

Immediately, I diverted my eyes and my mind away from his body to the floral arrangements.

"Pat," I said, "there aren't enough flowers here for David. These arrangements don't even look fresh." At that time, there were perhaps ten assorted wreaths on display. They looked as if they desperately needed water. Pat reminded me that these flowers had probably arrived as early as Monday.

I took in the music. A tape was playing very softly, on which I could hear David singing, "My Whole World Ended (the Moment You Left Me)." Memories of David standing up on stage after stage, singing that song, came flooding back. Still trying to keep my composure, I let my mind fade the music into the background.

"Tony," Pat asked, "Would you like to sit over here on the side? I'll have security bring you a chair."

They asked if they should stop the line so that I could have a few moments in private with David but I said, "No, you can keep the line going." I decided to read the cards on the floral arrangements instead.

Diana Ross had sent a very small, white bird of paradise arrangement—a somewhat chintzy affair that I was certain one of her staff people must have selected. Rod Stewart's display was huge and really quite hideous, as if his hairdresser might have created it. There was a sort of tropical-looking, Halloween type of thing from Hall and Oates positioned near the casket—Pat said it must have cost a fortune but I felt it was so awful, I didn't want to look at it. Another wreath was in the form of a huge gold record, trimmed with flowers. I was surprised to see Berry Gordy's flowers prominently placed right next to David's head.

All the while I was taking in the flowers, I kept sneaking glances at David, but my eyes were beginning to tear, and I couldn't make out his features clearly. All I could see were his trademark glasses. Then, when I was about six feet away from the casket, I really looked at him. I was shocked. I had heard that he hadn't been looking so good on the last tour, but now he looked almost perfect, as if he had been preparing himself for this event for months. His tuxedo was perfectly elegant. The crease in his pants was razor sharp. The shirt was crisp. I looked at his black patent-leather shoes with all the rhinestones. He looked like he was ready to go on stage and had just lain down for a minute's rest.

I looked more closely. Maybe he did seem a little drawn and thin. And the lips, as if he were trying to say something. The lips seemed a little flat, but I told myself, the embalmers never get the lips quite right.

A staff member from the funeral home unhooked the rope and I stepped right up to the casket. "David," I told him quietly, "you know that if you were dressed for a show and lay down in your tux, I would have had a fit." Usually I didn't even want the guys to sit, once they had their clothes on. "You have to stand like a soldier," I used to tell David. Sometimes he would get upset with me when I told him that: "If I put on these pants, and then I have to sit down to put on my show shoes, how am I supposed to keep the pants from wrinkling?"

I reached out and touched David's hand. I knew that it would feel ice cold. Then I leaned down to kiss his cheek, remembering how that used to feel, too.

The line was still streaming through but I just stood a while and watched him. He seemed so peaceful, so rested, so sharp—and not really like himself. I thought of all he meant to us, all the things that had been left unsaid. I sensed a kind of relief for David.

His songs filtered through the room and into my head again. We still had his voice.

On Sunday, Swanson's Funeral Home was still receiving endless crowds of people who wanted to view David's body. I spent most of the day resting at Pat's house, waiting for Eddie and Dennis to arrive. They had been previously booked for a Saturday night engagement and had gone ahead with it as planned, money being a factor as usual. Around five in the evening I checked in at the hotel. Eddie and Dennis had been given the presidential suites. Mine was just next door to Eddie's, where the caterers were already busying themselves with food and flowers, preparing the place for a wake.

Pat telephoned me from the lobby around seven o'clock, when everyone started arriving. I had not seen Eddie since the Super Bowl, and I had avoided calling him during those chaotic days of calls surrounding David's death. But whatever our problems had been, they seemed to have disappeared. I knew this when Eddie came right over to me and hugged me. He looked sullen, and thinner than I could ever remember him looking.

Eddie decided to go straight to the funeral home, and he told me he wanted to go alone. "After they settle in, Tony, tell everybody to come to my suite," he said. "There's dinner and soft drinks for everyone, but please save something for me. And Tony, don't let anyone do too much beer drinking. Keep everything cool and quiet, and don't let no one into my bedroom." I sensed that he wanted the group to stay close together tonight, like a family.

As soon as we'd gathered in Eddie's presidential suite everyone started talking about David. Our unspoken rule was, don't talk about the circumstances of death in front of Eddie. Although Eddie showed little emotion to us, we felt as if we knew what his real feelings were and we also knew how he tended to deal with his feelings. While we all hoped that sharing our memories of David with one another would help us bring him back to life long enough so that we could come to terms with his death, we didn't expect Eddie to join us. And we certainly didn't think Eddie would want to hear the one thing that everyone was saying over and over—that David Ruffin did not overdose himself.

"I think it was some of those people in the crack house. They knew he had all that money and they had probably given David dope on credit, and David probably didn't want to pay them. Somebody cooked up a rock he couldn't refuse."

"Maybe nobody was really trying to kill David," said Nate. "Maybe they were just trying to get him in a state where they could take the money without him resisting, and they went too far, and then when he collapsed they panicked."

Reports had emerged of autopsy photographs showing abrasions on David's chest and knees, as if he had been dragged. Nobody was quite sure what that might mean, but everybody agreed that if someone wanted to kill David Ruffin, the obvious method would be by drug overdose. Nobody would question it.

They put on videotapes of the group's recent European tour and showed me how great David had been in his last weeks, how clear his voice was, how he was looking better all the time.

"You know what David did?" Josie told me. One night in Europe, she said, they had come back to the hotel ravenously hungry, only to find the kitchen closed. David had opened up the hotel kitchen and, dressed only in his underwear and shoes, had proceeded to cook a complete meal for the whole crew.

"I believe it," I said. "That was David."

Before we knew it, Eddie was back, and the suite suddenly got quiet. We were acting like children around a father who has just lost his only child. I offered him food, but he wasn't hungry. He took off his jacket and lit his cigarette; he seemed shaken, but was trying to be very cool.

"Tony," he said, "I know you're not working, but would you mind unpacking some of my clothes so that I can change?" He was dressed in a finely tailored black suit.

"Eddie," I told him, "all of your clothes are already unpacked. They're hanging in your closet in the bedroom, and clothes for you to wear are laid out on your bed."

Silently, Eddie moved into the bedroom. I followed.

"Eddie, how do you think David looks?"

"I don't like how he looks."

"I figured you wouldn't."

"I think they've blown him up too much."

"Really?"

"Yeah, his lips and cheeks look too big. They've puffed him up too much. His head looks too big for his body."

"Well, they say that people's features change slightly every day after they're dead."

"I just don't like how he looks."

Ed was pacing around the bedroom. "You know," he finally said, "if I hadn't let David stay behind in London he wouldn't be dead now. He wouldn't have been carrying that money, and he wouldn't be dead."

I didn't answer him. There was no knowing what wrongs Eddie felt he had done David in all the years they'd been together. David hadn't made it easy for him, but I was sure that in his bereavement Eddie was now blaming himself for many things.

After changing, Eddie excused himself and went downstairs to the bandleader, Gary's suite. The rest of the staff stayed up trading favorite David Ruffin stories, watching performance videos, and consoling one another until about three in the morning. We had a couple of hours' sleep and then shared breakfast together before leaving, very early, for the funeral home. I had called there at around midnight to make arrangements for David Ruffin's background singers and band to have a private moment with him, and had been told that the public was still waiting on line.

When we got there around 9 A.M. the line was still very long. The Swanson's Funeral Home attendant was late in arriving, and when she did show up she was in a panic because David had to be at the church by ten o'clock and the line was still growing.

"I'm not letting them people on the line in," she told me. "There is no public viewing today."

She let us in and everybody gathered around David's open casket, and suddenly I realized how close we had all been. Josie lost it and completely broke down, and I was surprised to see the men, whom I had always seen as so totally cool, openly weeping. We hung around a bit, kind of reluctant to leave David there alone like that.

Meanwhile, fans on line outside were for the first time getting a little antsy, especially when the attendant went out there like Big Bad Mama to announce loud and clear, "There is no public viewing."

Baby, when that woman stood in front of that funeral home and told those people that there would be no viewing, the crowd went berserk. They ran across the lawn, right up to the front door: "We been here since six in the morning. We got to see David Ruffin. You crazy, woman?" And then all those people started screaming —the old ones, the young ones, the bourgeois ones, the homeless ones. They were ready to riot. Only when someone from the band said, "Miss, you better let them in!" did she very quickly announce, "Okay, when David Ruffin's staff leaves you may come in. But you'll have to walk very, very swiftly past the casket. There's to be no stopping."

The crowd calmed down instantly.

I watched them filing in before we left. The line was moving very fast and in a very orderly fashion. Nobody said much. I watched the line come in the front entrance and file past the body, and then I watched as people came out the back door and into the parking lot. Some people went in crying quietly, looked at David, and as soon as they got out into the parking lot they broke down and cried hysterically. Some of them collapsed on the ground.

We all truly loved David. He was our star, a legend, but he was also a man of the world, and a man of the street, touchable and approachable. People who were coming to see him for the final time identified with him in one way or another.

"I was in jail, too. I know what hell he went through."

"I'm an addict, I know what it is to get hooked. They shouldn't have put him in jail."

"David needed treatment, love, and affection, baby."

"Every one of us has a vice."

"Motown should have treated him better, and they should have never left Detroit."

"Anyway, I think he was murdered."

Some of them just loved him for his voice. "You don't judge people by the way they live their lives but by what they leave behind. And David Ruffin left beautiful music behind."

Over a four-day period a staggering number of fans and friends—maybe twenty thousand or so—filed past David's lean, lifeless body in that funeral home. Some just wanted to say good-bye to a man they had never even met, but felt they had known.

And on the ninth day after his death, David Eli Ruffin, "the Voice of the Temptations," was buried—but not without much ado.

None of us was quite prepared for what was to come. David's funeral service was to be held at the New Bethel Baptist Church on Franklin Boulevard—the church Aretha Franklin's father built. Having been to the funeral of ex-Supreme star Flo Ballard in 1976, I knew there would be a crowd of onlookers outside. But no one ever expected anything like what we saw as we approached the church in our convoy of stretch limos.

About ten long blocks away from the church I saw, from the limo's tinted windows, the first police barricades. Our limos sped through toward New Bethel Baptist, but all other traffic was virtually at a standstill. Mounted police were everywhere, holding the curious crowd back from the roadway on both sides. It was hard for anyone to move. It looked sort of like a crowd transplanted from the Macy's Thanksgiving Day parade, only without the festive smiles.

"What are these people doing?" I asked nobody in particular. "They're not going to hear or see anything."

The crowd got bigger and bigger as our limos approached the church, and the police presence got heavier—more mounted police, police on motorcycles, police on foot, police in cars. Finally, about a block away from the church, we had to leave the security of our limos and walk as a group under police protection.

I was walking right behind Eddie and Dennis, hoping that there would be no problems as we neared the front of the church, because the crowd was unbelievable. These were tough, die-hard, Motown-Temptations-David Ruffin fans who had either busted their way through ten blocks of crowd, or had gone straight to the church from the funeral home and waited all night. Some fans had even climbed up to the roof of a five-story building on the corner across from the church, and were sitting there with their feet just dangling over the edge. What we didn't know yet was that a whole crowd of devoted fans had already stampeded the church, screaming and trying to force their way into what was supposed to be a private funeral, but what would end up being a semiprivate affair as successive groups of fans were allowed in to sit in the balcony area for twenty minutes at a time. Meanwhile, those outside protested loudly that if it weren't for them, no stars would even be in that church.

As we strode into the church and down the center aisle, the reaction was only a little more restrained than the reaction outside had been. I could feel the intense heat as soon as I entered. The sanctuary was packed, and lined with what seemed to be about a hundred wreaths. Center front was the casket, open from head to toe.

The scene looked strangely like one big movie set. Television and still cameras were everywhere. We had to step over miles of cable to get down the center aisle, and then we had glaring spotlights shining in our faces. There were cameras focused right down on the casket, cameras peeking from between the wreaths, cameras looking down from the balcony, cameras trained on the stars who were already seated.

Eddie and Dennis walked straight up to the casket, past the ushers who were trying to quiet the crowd. They kissed David, and immediately a hush fell over the church—a hush broken only by the flashing of flashbulbs. Josie and I were next, followed by the male backup singers and the band. We were a tearful, close-knit family as we walked down the aisle to say our last farewell.

Aretha Franklin quietly told me where we were to be seated, and we made our way there. Just as we sat down the Four Tops arrived, looking very somber. Stevie Wonder was already in the church. Of course, Melvin Franklin and various other Temptations were in the house, as was Martha Reeves.

The Four Tops had just reached the casket when someone asked me, "Who is that dame with that horrible hair, up there at David's casket with Duke Fakir?" A short while later, Eddie and Dennis both turned around and stared at me curiously, so I leaned up and Eddie said to me, quietly, "Tony, don't you tell me you're not going to speak to Mary."

"What are you talking about? Mary who?"

"Mary Wilson."

"She's here?"

"She's right over there, in the fourth row behind Dennis's mother." Dennis told me that Mary had come over to me but that I had never even lifted my head. Honestly, I had not seen or heard her.

By this point Dennis and Eddie were glaring at me while the others looked on. "You should go and say something to Mary," Dennis told me. And I wanted to, only Dennis didn't know what I wanted to say. After all, this was the same Mary Wilson who had had me thrown out of a Beverly Hills bookstore that had booked us both for autograph sessions on my last book tour. So when the first opportunity arose I went over and gave her a polite hug and a Hollywood kiss, and that's when I realized that this was the dame with the "horrible hair," the woman whom we had seen standing at the casket with Duke Fakir of the Four Tops. I returned to my seat and sensed that Eddie and Dennis were now satisfied. I had acknowledged Mary: the family was intact.

An usher approached our group and asked if we would mind the Spinners sitting next to us. Nobody minded. But when the five men and their four, beefy bodyguards took their seats we were shocked to discover that these were not the Spinners, but Otis Williams and his Temptations. A hush fell over our group.

I looked around. This was, indeed, not your regular funeral crowd. It was more like a fashion show crossed with a costume party. People were dressed in bright red and vibrant oranges, greens, purples. There were the Mariah Carey wannabes in their microminis. There were a couple of black and white Madonnas, several Diana Ross clones in sequins, bugle beads, and hair. You had halter tops and bustiers, backless and sleeveless dresses, and men dressed in everything from *GQ* tux to jeans. I'm sure I wasn't the only one of David's friends to find the whole thing totally disrespectful.

I was just taking in the crowd when I saw two men in suits walk up to Eddie and whisper something in his ear. Eddie got up from his seat and left with the men. He came back shortly thereafter, and whispered something to Dennis. The men returned about ten minutes later. This time, Dennis said something to Josie before he too got up and left with Eddie and the men. I could see by the look on his face that something odd was going on. Josie whispered to me, "Tony, they're arresting Eddie."

"What!" I screamed. I'm a little excitable.

"They're arresting Eddie for child support."

As the funeral continued, I learned that the detectives had come to the funeral with a warrant for Eddie's arrest. He apparently owed twenty-six thousand dollars in back child support to his first wife, Pat. They had wanted to handcuff him and take him out right then and there, according to Dennis, but the Honorable Louis Farrakhan, who had asked to speak at the funeral, had intervened.

The whole thing with the police was handled very quickly and quietly in an upstairs office. According to Dennis, Minister Farrakhan told the detectives that if they dared to handcuff Eddie and take him out, he would personally go up to the podium and tell the whole church what was going on. The announcement would go out over the loudspeakers in the street. "You will never get this man out of the church," the Honorable Louis Farrakhan told the detectives.

Eddie was returned to his seat for the time being, and sat there cool as anything through most of the funeral, knowing that before it was all over he might be taken quietly out and directly to the judge's chamber.

Of course, we were all wondering why they had chosen the day of David Ruffin's funeral to arrest Eddie Kendrick on a warrant that was years old, when they'd had plenty of opportunities to arrest him in the past. One could only think that this had been done to embarrass Eddie, because at any other time this arrest would probably not have made the news. Who would want to embarrass Eddie?

I started wondering, Where's Nedra, where's the family? I couldn't see them anywhere. Meanwhile, the scene in the church was getting more and more out of hand, with crowds of people jamming the aisle, trying to get a last peek at David Ruffin in his casket.

Finally one of the church ladies—a vision in white—stood up at the podium and announced in her best church-lady voice, "I have several things to say. First of all, there will be no more viewing of the body by the general public unless you have one of New Bethel Church's validated parking passes. I ask all of the Moslem brothers who are here from the Nation of Islam and who have offered to help with security to check the passes. If you do not have a validated parking pass, please get off the line."

There were a lots of security guards from the Nation of Islam,

all impeccably groomed and dressed, and as they positioned themselves around the church everyone hushed up real quick.

Then the vision in white announced that David Ruffin's family
was still outside in the limos, afraid to set foot into the crowd that
was growing wilder by the minute. Would the brothers from the
Nation of Islam please help the family into the church?

With considerable protection from the Nation of Islam guards,
members of the Ruffin family finally entered the church. The guards
lined the aisle, allowing them unimpeded access to the casket. There
was a great deal of heavy weeping and wailing, and as they got
closer to David they started falling out.

It was a little later when the church lady spoke again. Tapping
on the mike for attention, she said, "Aretha . . . Aretha wants
. . . Aretha Franklin wants—the ushers are not doing what Aretha
said. Aretha wants the family taken care of, and the stars must be
taken care of. I want fans to be passed out. Please get these people
water—people are fainting. Usher board, please, I don't care how
hot it is, you must have on your full white uniform and your jackets.
We must show some respect in the house of the Lord. Now, see that
fans are passed out. We had a meeting about this, ladies."

"In addition, there has been an accident, there's no other way
to say it. There was a man, a guest, who has been hurt. The fans
outside pushed and shoved, stampeded the church's entrance on
Franklin Boulevard, north side of the building, and the man unfortunately lost part of his thumb in the door."

There was a hush, then a rumbling in the church.

"We need some assistance," continued the Vision in White.
"Will whoever came with this injured man please rise and go to the
back of the church where security is waiting for you. As you know,
we have ambulances on standby because we expected something
like this at the funeral of the great David Ruffin. The man's name
is—who came with John Hancock?"

As soon as she said that name a woman sitting in the middle of the church jumped up and let out a frightening scream. She shuffled past a whole pew of people and went rushing to the back while the church lady continued, "Now, I'm going to turn over the funeral to one of the brothers from the Nation of Islam. I'm relinquishing my duties at this time. Please be quiet." One of the ministers from the Nation of Islam stood up and the place grew still.

The minister calmly read the order of events, saying that due to time constraints and the huge number of speakers and soloists on the David Ruffin funeral program (which someone was now selling outside the church for ten dollars each) everybody would be limited to three minutes each.

A whole succession of singers and speakers now began to stand up at the podium, among them Berry's sister Esther Gordy, who spoke as her family's representative. Even from my seat up front, all I could see of her over the podium was her hat and what looked like a wig. Her speech really amounted to a lesson in Gordy family history, peppered here and there with mentions of David—how David had been helped by Berry Gordy after Gwen had signed him to her label, and how Berry Gordy was such a wonderful man and Berry had done this and Berry had done that and how Berry was a star maker and Berry was a genius and on and on, and the whole time I was trying not to chuckle because I had remembered a comment of David's: "Tony, that Gordy family makes the Borgias look like the Waltons."

In the middle of all this David Ruffin, Jr., fell out screeching and had to be taken out of the church shouting that he wanted to speak to Otis. And David's body lying out there in full view in a wide open casket only heightened the drama. People were getting so worked up that ushers had to stand around fanning them and serving cool water because there was so much heat being generated in there with all the carrying on that it felt hotter than you might imagine hell to be.

By the time Stevie Wonder stood at the podium, the mass hysteria was reaching a peak. He sang a song that he announced was from his latest album—an outpouring of love for David. He sang it so fabulously, with only acoustical accompaniment, that you could have heard a pin drop, and as soon as he was finished with this incredible wailing the congregation automatically rose to its feet and clapped. You would never have believed that this was a church, and that someone was being buried. I heard someone to my left mutter, "Where was Stevie Wonder when David Ruffin needed him? David could have definitely used a Stevie to write and produce a record for him."

Sometime during all this, they had closed the casket, but not before they had plucked David's black patent leather and rhinestone show shoes off his feet as normal as life—which generated more gasps and screams. They put a pair of regular patent leather shoes on his feet, and the show shoes were headed for a glass case in the Rock and Roll Hall of Fame.

From that point on things went completely haywire. Every few minutes there was another loud outburst, another standing ovation. You had a song, everybody rising to their feet, then you got a prayer followed by another song, then someone reading, somebody falling out, somebody being rushed out of the church. And through it all photographers were crowding to snap pictures, TV cameras were rolling into a shot, another prayer, another song. It was a carnival and a nightmare, and I would say that most of the people in that church were there to be seen or to gawk, and definitely to gossip.

There was a woman sitting right behind me who claimed to be a member of the church, and who didn't stop gossiping for about twenty-five minutes. "Yeah, girl, let me tell you a thing or two. The man was no good," she was saying to her friend. "David had at least four wives! Honey, my step-sister's girlfriend's cousin once told me that a friend of hers had known this woman that had lived with him. She said that he beat her ass! He was a big dopehead, took all her money, and almost made her lose her house up in Southfield, girl."

She kept on talking between choruses: "Baby, he gave her no money . . . Save me, precious savior . . . Let me tell you, girl, he had children all around the world . . . amen."

Finally I turned around and told her, "If you say one more incorrect word about David Ruffin, I'm going to turn back around and slap you in your face."

She left at once.

Eddie and Dennis had not been asked e   r to speak or sing at the funeral, and they had never thought to suggest it to the family because they wanted to be asked. So when it came time for the Temptations to take their three minutes in the funeral spotlight it was Melvin who went to the podium. Melvin had somehow been put in the position of representing both the Temptations and the family at the service, and of reading both eulogies, which we all thought was very odd. After all, Melvin had not worked with David for years.

As Melvin approached the podium Ollie Woodson got up, un-invited, and followed him. The whole time that Melvin was reading about how David was such a great singer, a wonderful character, a fabulous, legendary voice, Ollie was right there next to him, hanging tearfully over his shoulder and giving a whole dramatic show of his own.

When he had finally finished reading, Melvin called up his whole packet of Temptations and everybody applauded like crazy as they approached the podium, as if this were a music awards show. All of a sudden I saw a man vault down the aisle dressed in a gold Bermuda shorts set like you would wear to a Motown picnic. "Let him through," Melvin said when the Muslim guards stopped him. "He's cool. He's here to stand in for his cousin, the late Paul Williams." And the guy suddenly raised his hand in a black power salute.

Everybody in our group was looking at one another, shaking our heads, as if to say, Can you believe this? Can you believe this service? This bunch of lying bastards that couldn't stand David and called him every name in the book? We started wondering, What are Eddie and Dennis going to do if Melvin doesn't call them up to the podium?

Melvin had been up there a good while before he finally called Eddie Kendrick, at which point Eddie stood up amid thunderous applause, walked toward the podium, got halfway there, turned around to look at Dennis, who was still glued to his seat, and beckoned Dennis to join him. By this point Melvin was onto another subject—"Oh yeah," Melvin said quickly in his big bass voice. "You too. You're part of the Temptations too, Dennis."

So now you had almost everybody that was ever a part of the Temptations up there, plus a relative, all crowded around the podium. Melvin proudly announced that they were going to sing "My Girl," which I thought was an odd choice for a funeral. In my heart I knew that they had chosen it because this was a song that Ollie sang, and they wanted to have their best singer at bat to turn the whole place out.

Sure enough, Ollie stood at the mike and started singing and the crowd went crazy. I lowered my head in disgust. The next thing I knew, Dennis had pushed his way from the back to the podium, practically knocking Ollie out of the way, and was standing at the mike singing, "When it's cold outside, I got the month of May," in his best I'm-going-to-turn-this-mother-out gospel voice. He completely overshadowed Ollie. Then Ollie came back to the mike to get a few more lines in, at which point Dennis had to vocally finish Ollie off. It was a true, Motown-style vocal war between Dennis and Ollie, at the end of which the congregated mourners rose from their seats again to give yet another standing ovation.

By now the service had been going on for about four hours and it must have been a hundred-and-five degrees in there. I could hear the crowd in the street getting louder, when—"Ladies and gentlemen, Aretha Franklin."

Aretha got up slowly and walked down past the now closed

casket. As she reached the steps leading up to the podium, she stumbled slightly and everybody gasped, "Oh Aretha!" Visibly shaken, she said a few soft words about love and sadness, and then without any introduction she started to sing, her powerful voice growing increasingly more vibrant and more charged. Her eyes were closed, her head was thrown slightly back, and I could see tears rolling down her face. The whole church fell into a deep, trancelike hush. Even the organ that was accompanying Aretha died down almost to silence. It was pure voice ringing out within those stone walls. Aretha was singing in her daddy's church, and the people were listening, caught finally in the reality of why we were there. No one dared clap after Aretha had finished and been helped back to her seat.

Naturally, when the Honorable Louis Farrakhan stood up at the podium to give the closing remarks, the church started humming again. But the hum died down fast, because before he even started his sermon the minister laid into the crowd for the way they had been carrying on. The show was finally over.

What he basically said was, "All of you got what you came for. You came to take photographs, you came to see the stars. You people get up and leave now because although you need to hear what I'm going to say, you probably won't understand it anyway.

"All you women who are here talking about how you can't find a decent black man because all the black men are in jail, all the black men are on dope—look at yourselves and the clothes you women came in. Even if this were a wedding, a joyous occasion, you do not enter the House of the Lord like that. All you women need to get up and get out of here with your sleeveless and backless costumes. I don't have to point you out, you know who you are."

The church started emptying out in a hurry, and if anyone didn't get up fast enough they were being told to get up. "You in the eighth row, please. Come on, sister, get up. You don't come in here like that."

I wanted to turn around and look at who was leaving but you didn't even want to blink while Minister Farrakhan was speaking, and he had now begun.

"David could buy things, but he could not buy happiness," he said. He claimed that David Ruffin had once called him to say that he was being held captive in Arizona by some thugs from an unnamed major record company, and that he desperately needed help. "He was reaching out for help." A few weeks later, when Minister Farrakhan had finished a road tour and tried to reach David, David could not be reached.

"He was more than a song, more than an entertainer. He was a divine being put in flesh and blood that has left from among us. But we who are left behind must not just clap our hands and weep and mourn, for he is out of trouble. You are still in it."

The stars you like to look up at, the Honorable Louis Farrakhan told the crowd, are some of the most miserable people in the world. These people are nothing. They are the new slaves. These people, he said, have been through so much misery—they've been robbed, they've been abused, they've been enslaved. "These people are in hell. You don't know the trouble they've got."

He spoke the truth.

The Vision in White called for the flower bearers to line up in the center aisle, and as they did I watched them struggle toward the exit with the huge wreaths. It took four people to carry some of those things out. Then came the two funeral directors dressed in white top hats and tails, carrying canes. With one marching in front and one behind, they ushered the casket up the center aisle. Serving as pallbearers were, of course, the Temptations minus Eddie Kendrick, who by now was on his way to meet the judge.

Fortunately, Martha Reeves averted a tragic conclusion to a tragic day. She placed a call to Berry Gordy and told him that ten thousand dollars was needed for Eddie's bail. The money was there in no time.

Later I told Eddie, "Isn't that something, Berry Gordy paying your bail so quick!"

"It's nothing but some of my money back that he stole from me," said Eddie bitterly. "He stole more than that from all of us in a day."

Once again, it all came back to Big Daddy Berry Gordy. It wasn't just the stolen money that made Eddie bitter. He was bitter because, after all these years, he was still dependent on a man he detested to bail him out. Like so many other ex-Motowners, Eddie had come to Motown with nothing, and he had left with even less—because he had left part of his soul behind.

Epilogue

On July 10, 1991, at six o'clock in the morning, I caught my reflection in the lobby mirror as I left the hotel in Amsterdam. I winked at myself—a knowing wink, because finally I felt myself delivered from the temptation to hold on. I felt as if I'd been delivered from a cult. I had decided to quit the former Temptations. Little did I know that Eddie, meanwhile, had decided to dump me. He never actually fired me—I just never heard from him again after this tour. July 1991 was the last time I ever worked with a Temptation.

This was the end of a short tour, as tours go. It had been billed, deceitfully, as "The Reunion of the Temptations, featuring Eddie Kendrick and Dennis Edwards." We had all left the States en route for Paris late one evening in June, just days after laying David Ruffin to rest. Emotionally shaken, we had made our way by air and bus through France, Belgium, Austria, Spain, Italy, and Yugoslavia. No place was too risky for an invincible Temptation—not even Yugoslavia, a country torn by civil war—and no bus trip was too arduous. Sometimes we'd be in that tour bus eighteen or twenty-four hours straight. By the time the tour's last performance ended on the Museum Stage in Amsterdam, I was suffering from a bad flu and felt headed for my first heart attack.

It had been a debilitating experience, this last tour—not because of the usual mayhem, but because suddenly the reality behind the legend was becoming all too clear to me. Maybe it was dawning on Eddie too. Even at fifty-something, Eddie still cut a dashing figure. But beneath that charm was a growing cynicism that was eating him up inside, and sharpening a vicious tongue.

"You motherfuckin' bitch, are you crazy? This is my tour bus and my goddamn show!"

I had never, ever, heard Eddie talk like this before to anybody. It was the middle of the night on the tour bus, and I had just asked him to lower the volume on a wild Screamin' Jay Hawkins tape he'd woken us all up with.

"Well, people are trying to sleep," I told him.

"I'll put your fuckin' ass off the bus, you damn tramp! You don't talk to *me* like that!"

As a member of the former Temptations' staff I had been programmed to disregard this kind of thing. After all, Eddie was a star, a legend, and we all make excuses for legends. He'd held on long—awfully long—outliving fellow original Temptations David Ruffin and Paul Williams. He'd watched the self-destruction and deaths of two of his closest friends, and had taken a lesson from both. The lesson was, don't get caught up in it. Setting himself apart, he'd survived despite the massive ups and downs of his career. And now he was bent on holding on, even though there was hardly anything left to hold on to now beyond the legend.

Eddie thought he was the one holding it all together, just like Otis Williams was holding together his bunch of Temptations. But the one who was really keeping the situation from careening off the rails now was Dennis Edwards. When he heard Eddie's outburst on the bus that night he got up and told me, "Tony, go to your bed." Then he snapped up skinny little Eddie, dragged him down the aisle, and literally threw him up into his berth.

As the tour progressed and Eddie Kendrick grew nastier and nastier, Dennis became a solid buffer between Eddie and the rest of the crew. He defended the background singers when Eddie accused them of singing better behind Dennis than they sang behind him, and dancing better behind Dennis than they danced behind him. I wondered if Dennis had finally come out from behind the shadow of David Ruffin and found his own strength.

By the time we reached Amsterdam, Eddie wasn't talking to anyone—he was in his silent-treatment mode. But we just let it go. After all, he was suffering remorse and grief, or so we guessed. Who knew? Eddie never even mentioned David during that entire tour. It was like, Who was David Ruffin? We tiptoed around Eddie and forgave him for his belligerent behavior, just like we used to suffer the verbal abuse David threw at us when he was in the mood. They were stars, legends, and if they needed to abuse us so they could magnify themselves and their own stardom, then we were ready and willing. After all, we wanted to work for the stars because that made us stars, too.

Motown had taught its stars to expect the best, and we had been taught to give them the best—to fuss over them, to idolize them, to watch their every move and make sure that nothing happened to upset them. If a star orders pizza, make sure he gets it hot, because cold pizza could throw him into a tizzy, and God forbid—Motown couldn't afford a star in a tizzy.

Everything had to be perfect. We had to be perfect. We had to speak, dress, and act perfectly for our stars because they were special. They were worth millions to the company. We learned to hold on to our jobs by playing along so we could keep eating the crumbs that fell off the stars' tables—so we could keep on being stars. Even if you just shined the Temptations' shoes, you tried to do it perfectly because you didn't want to end up shining the Contours' shoes.

We became victims of abuse, but we were also participants in our stars' infinite vanity—the vanity that made them legends. We let them believe in their own publicity. We let them believe they were something extra-extra-special, that they were demigods and nothing could touch them and nothing bad was supposed to happen to them, and if it did, somebody was going to rescue them. We were all playing the game together, without understanding how destructive it was.

I knew it as I stood in that Amsterdam hotel lobby, and it became crystal clear twenty-four hours later as I told my friend Charles tour horror stories on the way home from the airport. I knew I'd become an eager participant in the legend that Berry Gordy had spun out of Detroit, tempted by the same dream that Berry Gordy used to tempt all those young, would-be stars into taking a bite out of Motown's apple without ever looking for worms. After all, why worry? This was a family, and families are there to protect, not to exploit. Motown offered salvation through stardom.

I thought about the old Motown "family," with Big Daddy Berry Gordy sheltering his stable from all outside influences—including outside lawyers, outside accountants, outside lovers—and controlling every move. Like Otis Williams has said, "All we had to do was show up and sing." With its atmosphere of secrecy and its encouragement of dependency, Motown was almost a cult. Performers like the Temptations were programmed by the company to look good, sing well, say the right things, take what was offered, and ask no questions. They learned that success lay in loyalty to the family. And they were taught to trust and believe in the power of the company to take care of their every need or desire. Then they started to see that Berry Gordy was no daddy, this was no fatherly love, that the man was treating them like so many other managers and promoters and record company bosses might. When they started to see that, they found out that they were powerless to change the course of their lives because Berry Gordy controlled them, and if he wanted to punish them by keeping them on the back burner for years until their contract that they never really understood ran out, then there was nothing they could do about it.

I started to understand why, even years later, when they were middle-aged men with grandchildren and graying hair, David, Eddie, and Dennis blamed Motown and Berry Gordy for everything that went wrong with their lives. Victims of the cult mentality on which Gordy had bred them, they couldn't stop thinking of that fabulous nirvana that they thought he had taken away from them, but which was really Berry Gordy's dreamland all along. Berry Gordy's dreamland consisted of all these little elves, like Marvin Gaye, Flo Ballard, Martha Reeves, Mary Wells, Diana Ross, the Supremes, the Temptations, who ran around doing things for the king, financing his dream and his present Walt Disney World lifestyle. But very few of them, after being integral parts of Gordy's dream, and then being exiled from it in one way or another, learned how to reproduce the dream for themselves.

It boggles my mind why in the hell legendary entertainers like Eddie Kendrick, Dennis Edwards, and the late David Ruffin seem to have never recovered from the atrocities they claim were committed against them at Motown, but instead seem to lean on the memories like on a crutch.

So, as you see, the tragic and shocking story of the Temptations and Motown was hardly like a dream. However, when I happened upon that dreamland, I was young; and through it, became wise. I was a virgin, but because of it became experienced. I was willingly

and effectively programmed, but in spite of it became knowledge-
able. And only now, I confess, do I begin the process of understanding it.

For me, this dreamland is no longer a thrill. I am delivered from
the temptation to continue the ride, especially since the rides were
never free. I paid my fare, I had my fun—now I'm leaving the park.

Once, it was all right.

About the Author

Tony Turner was born in New York City. Always enterprising and adventurous, he was only twelve years old and living in a Harlem housing project when by chance he met and became the young confidant to Florence Ballard of the Supremes. From that encounter on, Motown, Berry Gordy, and his Motown stable of superstars became the central focus of Tony's life.

An astute youngster, Tony first worked as a gofer and, far more importantly, has been an insider since the early days at Motown. After attending college, he returned to the music business, working with some of Motown's greats—including the Supremes, Martha and the Vandellas, and most recently David Ruffin, Dennis Edwards, and Eddie Kendrick, formerly of the Temptations.

In 1990 Tony Turner saw his first book, *All That Glittered: My Life with the Supremes*, released to critical acclaim. It was the riveting tell-all, firsthand truth, that both Diana Ross and Mary Wilson tried unsuccessfully to suppress.

Today, he is writing his third book, as well as working on a live television talk show, "Tony Turner Talks." Tony divides his time between homes in New York and on the Gulf of Mexico.

Index

A

"Ain't Too Proud to Beg," [the Temptations], 11

All That Glittered: My Life with the Supremes (Tony Turner), 2–3, 99, 108

Apollo Theater, the, 77–92, 107

Atkins, Cholly, 13

Atlantic Records, 45

B

Ballard, Florence, 5–6, 11, 14–16, 23, 36, 189, 241;
  death of, 223;
  leaves the Supremes, 28–29, 33, 43, 77

Bannister, Billy, 63, 66, 68

Benson, Obie (Renaldo), 58

Birdsong, Cindy, 29, 98

"Boogie Down," [Eddie Kendrick], 43